Ken Jenkins hooks us by first sharing
resilience. He then takes us on a jour
resilience of survivors of airline cra
sharing his experience and integrating the dos and don'ts of traumatic
event response, but also taking us into the mind of the care team
responder. There he shares first-hand the psychological and emotional
experiences of working with survivors, and also coming to know the
victims of traumatic events through their families. This is a must read
for all traumatic event response team members.

Steve L. Whatley, Ph.D.
Retired Police Sergeant & Crisis Interventionist
Leadership Coach • Organization Consultant

During my career I've conducted accident investigations on behalf
of the U.S. Navy, the National Transportation Safety Board, and
American Airlines. From 1995 till 2003 I was in charge of accident
investigations at American Airlines. Prior to American Airlines my
accident investigation experience was totally on the technical and
operational side. While at American I was quickly and fully exposed
to the family assistance challenges of aircraft accidents. It proved to
be an eye-opening experience; fortunately for me, Ken Jenkins and
others like him were there to get us through those challenges.

I've always had a problem with academic folks who write books
and teach classes about things they've never done. They've read and
researched but they've never walked the walk. This book's credibility
is established by the experience of its author, Ken Jenkins. I lived
through several of the accidents referenced in this book. I saw Ken,
along with his peers, struggle as they assisted family and friends of
accident victims. The human experiences shared in this book are real
and few people can tell this story.

If you're going to read one book on post-accident family assistance
this is the one to read. You will not find another author with more
experience and knowledge on this topic than Ken Jenkins.

Tommy McFall
Aircraft Accident Investigation,
Reconstruction, and Expert Witness

RESILIENCE

Stories of Courage and Survival in Aviation Disasters

KEN JENKINS

Resilience
Stories of Courage and Survival in Aviation Disasters

Published by:
SEGR Publishing
Grapevine, TX USA
www.SEGRPublishing.com

Edited by: Heidi Clingen
www.allwritey.com
Final edit and proofreading by: Elaine Bellamore Phillips
Cover design by Andrea Ferguson
www.320designs.com

Library of Congress Control Number: 2014953894

Photos provided by:
National Transportation Safety Board
Michael L Dransfield, Flight 102 photos
AP Images

ISBN: 978-1-61920-036-4

Dedication

This book is dedicated to the victim's families, who after losing their loved one(s) so tragically, I was privileged to assist. Their spirit of survival, resilience and empathy continue to inspire me today.

Contents

Preface

In the 1980's and 1990's, there were a number of high profile accidents, which would bring the topic of airline family assistance to the forefront of the news. Events and accidents such as the bombing of Pan Am Flight 103, US Air Flight 5050, US Air Flight 405, US Air Flight 427, American Eagle Flight 4184, ValuJet 592 and TWA 800. According to families, there were a number of shortcomings with how airlines responded in the aftermath of these disasters which only made the loss of their loved one even worse.

This led to the creation of family advocacy groups, which in turn, lobbied Congress for legislation to change how airlines should, and would, respond in the aftermath of a disaster. Because of the strength, courage and resilience of these survivors and family members, The Aviation Disaster Family Assistance Act of 1996 (The Act) was signed by President Bill Clinton on September 6, 1996.

The Act was designed to ensure a coordinated response from the necessary stakeholders such as the airline having the accident, the National Transportation Safety Board (NTSB) the American Red Cross (ARC), the Department of State (DOS) as well as a number of other agencies. In addition, The Federal Family Assistance Plan For Aviation Disasters specifies Victim Support Tasks (VSTs) for seven organizations to perform in the aftermath of an air disaster (www.ntsb.gov). The Act gave permission to the aviation industry to talk about accidents, specifically, how to respond to them.

The goal, provide information and access to services for families and survivors, as quickly as possible and to reduce the second assaults similar to the ones family members and survivors of accidents had previously experienced.

Until The Act was signed in 1996, most airlines simply had family assistance plans written within their policies and procedures manual. To my knowledge there was not a formal, active educational training program within the airline industry until American Airlines began their family assistance program in 1993. What I do know, is the survivors and family members of aviation accidents spoke loud and clear. Something had to change in the way airlines responded to an accident. Today, there is some form of aviation family assistance legislation in Australia, Brazil, China, the European Union, Korea, and the United Kingdom. In addition, the International Civil Aviation Organization (ICAO) and the International Air Transport Association (IATA) have policy documents and guidelines regarding family assistance in aviation disasters.

For over 20 years, I have witnessed the resilience and perseverance of victims' family members and survivors who have chosen to use their personal experience to enhance post-crisis management policy and procedures for future aviation accident victims and their families. I have been privileged to work with many of these individuals over the years and am grateful for their dedication to the post-crisis management and family assistance. They are a true testimony to resilience, courage and survival.

Acknowledgements

If it were not for family, I would not be able to do the work I do. For the families I have served, thank you for allowing me the opportunity to serve during such a tragic time. Your strength, resolve, warmth and graciousness, were and are, gifts to the spirit of human resiliency. Thank you!

For my family, thank you for never ending support. We have each experienced tragedies and our faith in God, family, humor and determination have seen us through difficult times. Survival definitely describes our family! Thank you, Lorraine, for your patience and willingness to work with me on this endeavor. You have a very sharp eye. Larry, you show me how to keep going even when it seems like we shouldn't. For my partner, David, thank you for your belief in me. Most of all, thank you for always being willing to listen when I needed to talk. Most of all, I would like to thank my mother. She was the true example of resilience and survival. I love you Mom and I miss you every day.

A special thank you to my Angels. What a blessing to work and respond with such compassionate, caring, professional individuals. I will never be able to express how much you mean to me.

Introduction

From the time I was a little boy I wanted to be a lawyer. I competed in speech, debate, and extemporaneous speaking contests in school. I studied British Constitutional Law and Political Science. Everything I did was in preparation to become a lawyer. Then I decided to travel the world for a year before going to law school. I went to work for American Airlines (AA). However, the allure of the fast-paced and exciting airline business was difficult to pull away from. American Airlines was growing and providing opportunities for advancement so I stayed…longer than I initially thought I would.

Working for American Airlines changed the trajectory of my life. Instead of burying myself in legal tomes, I initially worked in Reservation Sales, then in Airport Operations before moving into Human Resources as a management analyst.

Early in my career with American my grandfather and my father died within a few months of each other. Soon thereafter my brother committed suicide. When the Medical Examiner (M.E.) called my mother and asked her if she was alone she replied, "Yes. Just tell me which one of my children is dead." Our family had experienced three deaths in nine months. My mother was as courageous as she was resilient. She was strong, having grown up in England during World War II. While grieving the family losses, she kept all of us together with her strength and sense of humor. Thankfully, those traits run in my family. For example, when my brother's funeral service was scheduled, my nephew wondered aloud, "What do we wear that no one has seen us wear over the past few months?" I tried not to smile but I couldn't help myself. Nervously, the smile turned into a laugh. I was grateful when my sister and my mother started to laugh, too. At that moment, we all knew we would somehow survive our grief.

Later in my career, through a series of events you will discover in this book, I landed in the Safety Department. I was home. I immersed myself in learning about Emergency Response Planning (ERP), Safety Management Systems (SMS), Aviation Safety Action Program (ASAP), Flight Operations Quality Assurance (FOQA), and Human Factors. As a result of my fascination, I went to graduate school and earned a master's degree in Aeronautical Science (MAS with Distinction) from Embry-Riddle Aeronautical University.

In March 1993, I was invited by the American Airlines Passenger Assistance Command Center (PACC) to attend a two-day seminar on family assistance. The airline realized, while aviation accidents were rare, it was a good idea to have employees trained to respond to accidents if and when they did occur. The facilitators assured us we would never have to use this training.

In the seminar we learned how to recognize and respond to traumatic stress, to "conduct a death notification," and to maintain our own emotional resilience during and after a deployment.

Little did I know my experiences would serve me so well. Over the next ten years, from 1994-2004, American Airlines, American Eagle and their partner carrier, American Connection, would have a horrifying total of eight fatal events. I was on the front lines in responding to each of them.

Shocking and traumatic events affect everyone uniquely. I know this because I have assisted families of airline crash victims for more than twenty years. I have witnessed a wide spectrum of courageous grief and resilience. I grew to love the sense of purpose of disaster response and the opportunity to be of service during tragic situations. I had no idea disaster response work would become my life's calling and purpose.

This book is the story of what I learned about disaster response, survival, and the resilience of the human spirit.

American Airlines Flight 102

Dallas / Fort Worth Airport, Texas

April 14, 1993

N 1993 I WAS WORKING as a financial analyst for the American Airlines Employee Suggestion Program, IdeAAs In Action. At the time, my background was comprised of management in Human Resources, Airport Operations as a Passenger Service Instructor and Reservation Sales Agent. One day, in my company mailbox, I received an invitation to participate in a new training program called The Passenger Assistance Command Center (PACC). The program was designed to educate employee volunteers on how to help passengers who were injured or who survived an accident, or, to assist families of those who died in an aviation accident.

I don't know why I received the invitation but knew the program sounded worthwhile and I was eager to serve my company. I completed the lengthy application, which asked questions regarding my experiences with loss. How did I handle it? What was my reaction to the loss? As well as many other questions on how I dealt with stress. I submitted my application and waited to hear if I had been accepted into the class.

Having been with the company for eleven years, I had a strong sense of pride working for American Airlines. It is one of the larger employers in the Dallas/Fort Worth area. I wanted to help our passengers if something went wrong. My application was accepted and I was scheduled to attend class.

There were approximately 20-25 employees and two facilitators in the class, which started in early March 1993. We were asked to complete a short quiz on the pre-work material we had been asked to read before we came to class and then settled in to the agenda of topics we would cover over the next two days.

Our facilitators explained: while AA had a response plan in our Rules and Regulations Manual, there had never been any formal Family Assistance training by airlines until now. There was no Federal legislation, Family Assistance Center or briefings to family members from accident investigators. However, I am getting ahead of myself. More about those functions later.

We watched videos of employees who had assisted family members of victims of AA Flight 191, a horrific accident at Chicago's O'Hare Airport (ORD) in 1979. This accident is noted today as one of the worst aviation tragedies in U.S. history. As each employee spoke about how they responded I was captivated how each simply wanted to help people during a difficult situation. An opportunity to give back was all I needed to join. The training session was educational and emotional. Our facilitators said we could practice and incorporate what we were learning in our personal and professional lives because it was unlikely we would ever have the opportunity to use it in an accident because they are rare. They were wrong!

Two or three weeks after the PACC class, I was attending a departmental staff meeting. Someone came to the room asking for me. I excused myself from the meeting and was advised PACC was being activated due to an aircraft off the runway at Dallas/Fort Worth International Airport (DFW). The 60 or so PACC team members were briefed of the event. We were told AA Flight 102 from Honolulu (HNL) to DFW, a DC-10 aircraft, hydroplaned off the runway. The nose gear collapsed and, when the plane came to a stop, the crew initiated an emergency evacuation. We were advised a number of passengers were injured while evacuating the aircraft and were sent to local area hospitals. In addition, due to the rain, the passengers needed dry clothes. Thankfully there were no deaths.

We were told some of us would be partnered with another PACC member and assigned to a passenger. There were not enough team members to pair a male with a female and we certainly did not have the opportunity to pair experienced with inexperienced as we had all just recently been trained. My PACC partner was a male and we were assigned to a male passenger who had been injured in the evacuation. We were asked to go to the hospital where the passenger had been

Flight 102

PHOTO BY: Michael L Dransfield

admitted to introduce ourselves and explain our role and provide any necessary assistance.

The passenger was a young man, possibly in his late 20's or early 30's. He was very nice and appreciative of our assistance. My PACC partner and I introduced ourselves to the doctor and charge nurse. We provided the hospital administration with a phone number and an address where the medical bill could be sent and where they could ask questions they may have had regarding payment. We also set about finding our passenger some dry clothes to wear.

We performed many activities during our three to four day deployment. Overall, we ensured our passenger was informed about the logistics of continuing his flight once the doctor released him from the hospital. We told him the cost was being taken care of by American

Flight 102

PHOTO BY: Michael L Dransfield

Airlines. In addition, we provided him with the phone number of Corporate Insurance/Risk Management should he have additional questions after he returned home.

An added note about Flight 102 — quite a few passengers were ready to continue to their final destination if they could change into dry clothes. The authorities had not released the luggage from the flight so the PACC members purchased almost all the clothes in the various gift shops for the passengers to wear. To say the least, most were dressed in Dallas Cowboys football and Texas Rangers baseball fan wear. I was surprised so many passengers wanted to continue their travel. I remember thinking what a close call this was for American and how fortunate there were no fatalities.

Flight 102

PHOTO BY: Michael L Dransfield

Several days after the last passenger was released from the hospital and continued on their trip, several of the PACC members were asked to make outbound phone calls, from the airlines Telephone Enquiry Center (TEC) to the passengers of Flight 102. We were to check on their well-being and to see if they had any questions or required any additional medical services. The phone calls were very well received and most were very appreciate of the assistance PACC provided.

A few weeks after the activation was complete, all the PACC members who responded met to debrief from an operational perspective. We talked about what worked well, what did not and where should changes be made. Everything about the response seemed matter of fact. Yes, we were all nervous. Yes, we were charting new territory but, for the most part, everything was going as we had been trained. I also realized how important this team was going to be if something more serious happened. I also realized I was up to the task to help. I just had no idea how many more times we would be called to do so.

Flight 102

PHOTOS BY: Michael L Dransfield

Flight 102

PHOTOS BY: Michael L Dransfield

Flight 102

PHOTOS BY: Michael L Dransfield

Lessons Learned

There were many lessons learned during the first activation of PACC. I have listed several of the key points we learned from the short activation of Flight 102.

1   **Be prepared.** The facilitators said we would never have to use the program. They were wrong. Prepare for the worst case scenario and be prepared to respond.

2   **Determine in advance the level of events your team will respond to.** The initial intent of PACC was to respond to a fatal situation. However, flexibility is key. There may be events such as Flight 102 where the team needs to be deployed even when there are no fatalities.

3   **Secure line of credit options at local retailers.** You never know when you will need to procure clothes for 200+ people at a moments notice. Establish relationships with key retailers before you need their assistance or everyone will be wearing local baseball and football team logo wear.

4   **Invest in technology.** Mobile and satellite phones, laptop computers and other essential technology are critical for quickly responding to a disaster.

5   **Build relationships with the local trauma hospitals in your area.** If your employees or customers could be sent to their hospital, it is better to know who the key stakeholders are at each hospital now. This will prove invaluable when it comes time for payment of services.

Flight 102

Executive Summary

On April 14, 1993, about 0659:43 central daylight time, American Airlines flight 102, a McDonnell Douglas DC-10-30, departed runway 17 left, following landing at Dallas/Fort Worth International Airport, Texas, after a nonstop, overnight flight from Honolulu International Airport, Hawaii. It was raining at the time of the landing, and there were numerous thunderstorms in the area. There were 189 passengers, 3 flightcrew members and 10 cabincrew members aboard the airplane. Two passengers received serious injuries, and 35 passengers, 1 flightcrew member, and 2 cabincrew members received minor injuries during the evacuation of the airplane. The airplane sustained substantial damage.

The National Transportation Safety Board determines that the probable cause of the accident was the failure of the captain to use proper directional control techniques to maintain the airplane on the runway.

The safety issues in this report focused on weather conditions affecting the flight, flightcrew and air traffic control training and procedures, airplane emergency evacuation lighting, and runway maintenance.

Safety recommendations concerning these issues were addressed to the Federal Aviation Administration, Dallas/Fort Worth International Airport, and American Airlines, Inc.

Flight 102

National Transportation Safety Board
Washington, DC 20594

Brief of Accident

Adopted 12/27/1994

Printed on : 11/23/2014 06:16:31 PM

DCA93MA040
File No. 388

04/14/1993   DALLAS/FT WORTH, TX   Aircraft Reg No. N139AA   Time (Local): 07:00 CDT

Make/Model: Douglas/DC-10-30
Engine Make/Model: Ge / CF6-50C2
Aircraft Damage: Substantial
Number of Engines: 3
Operating Certificate(s): Flag Carrier/Domestic
Name of Carrier: AMERICAN AIRLINES
Type of Flight Operation: Scheduled; Domestic; Passenger Only
Reg. Flight Conducted Under: Part 121: Air Carrier

	Fatal	Serious	Minor/None
Crew	0	0	13
Pass	0	2	187

Last Depart. Point: HONOLULU, HI
Destination: Same as Accident/Incident Location
Airport Proximity: On Airport/Airstrip
Airport Name: DALLAS/FT WORTH INTL
Runway Identification: 17L
Runway Length/Width (Ft): 11388 / 150
Runway Surface: Concrete
Runway Surface Condition: Wet

Condition of Light: Day
Weather Info Src: Unknown
Basic Weather: Instrument Conditions
Lowest Ceiling: 900 Ft. AGL, Overcast
Visibility: 1.50 SM
Wind Dir/Speed: 300 / 022 kts
Temperature (°C): 19
Precip/Obscuration:

Pilot-in-Command   Age: 59

Certificate(s)/Rating(s)
Airline Transport; Commercial; Multi-engine Land; Single-engine Land

Instrument Ratings
Airplane

Flight Time (Hours)

Total All Aircraft: 12562
Last 90 Days: Unk/Nr
Total Make/Model: 555
Total Instrument Time: UnK/Nr

*** Note: NTSB investigators traveled in support of this investigation and used data obtained from various sources to prepare this aircraft accident report. ***

AT THE TIME FLIGHT 102 LANDED AT DFW AIRPORT, IT WAS RAINING AND THERE WERE NUMEROUS THUNDERSTORMS IN THE AREA. SHORTLY AFTER TOUCHDOWN ON RUNWAY 17 LEFT, THE PILOT LOST DIRECTIONAL CONTROL WHEN THE AIRPLANE BEGAN TO WEATHERVANE AND THE CAPTAIN FAILED TO USE SUFFICIENT RUDDER CONTROL TO REGAIN THE PROPER GROUND TRACK. THE AIRPLANE EVENTUALLY DEPARTED THE RIGHT SIDE OF THE RUNWAY. AT THE TIME OF LANDING THE WIND (A CROSS WIND) WAS BLOWING AT 15 KNOTS WITH GUSTS APPROXIMATELY 5 KNOTS ABOVE THE STEADY WIND SPEED.

Simmons Airlines 4184
DBA American Eagle

Roselawn, Indiana
October 31, 1994

I T WAS THE FIRST HALLOWEEN in my new house in Grapevine, TX. I was excited about getting home so I could hand out candy to the trick-or-treaters and see all the different Halloween costumes. The drive home from work was slow because of heavy traffic. I was listening to the news when I heard an airplane, destined for Chicago, had crashed in Indiana. The airline, type of plane and number of people on board was not provided as those details had yet to be determined. I felt bad for what had happened and for a brief moment wondered if it was one of American's planes.

As I continued listening to the news as I drove, I learned American Eagle Flight 4184 flying from Indianapolis, IN (IND) to Chicago, IL (ORD) had crashed in Roselawn, IN. There were two pilots, two flight attendants and 64 passengers on board the aircraft. My excitement of Halloween night quickly changed from anticipation to a sick feeling in my stomach.

I honestly cannot say what time I finally arrived home but it was nearly dark. Kids were walking around the neighborhood in their costumes going door-to-door trick-or-treating while their parents stood back keeping an eye on them. I quickly checked my voicemail to see if anyone from the Customer Assistance Relief Effort (CARE) Command Center had called but there was no message. The PACC team had morphed into the CARE Team some time after the Flight 102 accident in 1993. CARE Team members had been advised in training class not to call in, because, during an emergency, things would be quite hectic. We were to be patient and wait for the call from Headquarters (HDQ). I put the Halloween candy in a bowl and proceeded to answer the door when the bell rang. Halloween was not as much fun as I thought it would be.

During the evening I spoke to my spouse and called my family to tell them about the accident and that I may have to leave for a few weeks. It is crucial you talk to your own family before you leave on assignment. It is important they understand the type of service you will provide and how emotional it may be for you. They need to know you may not always have time or the energy to call home every day. You may come home to find you are not the same person you were before you left. Responding to such a traumatic event may cause you to rethink your priorities in life. Your response to a mass casualty accident is life changing not only for those involved in the accident, but for their families and for you, too.

The front porch light was off now, no more trick-or treaters for the night. I watched the evening news at 10:00 p.m. The news reports were not good and they confirmed American Eagle Flight 4184 had crashed in Roselawn, IN. Newscasters reported there were no survivors. The weather in the Chicago area was cold and wet. There was already a great deal of speculation the weather contributed to the accident. How could anyone know so soon after the crash? I found myself asking how this could happen? Was I going to be activated or were local Chicago employees going to handle the response? I assumed Chicago would handle the crisis since it was a large hub with thousands of employees in the area. I could not sleep as my mind raced through so many random thoughts.

The next morning I went to work and many members of CARE were calling each other to see if anyone had heard from CARE HDQ. Some had, some had not. I was contacted by someone from CARE Command in the mid-afternoon and was asked if I was available for deployment. I said I would help in any way possible. I was told I would be flying to Chicago to work with the husband of a passenger who had been on board the plane. The CARE leader provided me the passenger's name I would be assigned to and the contact information of the husband. Once my flight arrangements had been made, I was asked to call the husband to introduce myself and to schedule our first meeting. I called the passenger's home and introduced myself. I offered my condolences regarding the accident and explained I was on my way to Chicago to meet with him personally and to answer questions he may have. I advised him my flight to ORD was going to arrive around 7:00 p.m. I asked him if he would like me to call him when I arrived in Chicago and he said yes. I quickly advised my manager I was being deployed, went home to pack and made my way to the airport. I did not know who I would be partnered with but would find out in ORD. During my flight I read our team member manual and reviewed key sections explaining the various activities we may be asked to facilitate.

Upon my arrival in ORD I immediately went to the CARE Command Center, which was located in Terminal H, ramp level at O'Hare Airport. Several offices and a conference room had been vacated for CARE to use in the response. I was briefed on a multitude of logistical topics and advised my CTM partner would not be arriving until the next day. The team members in the command center were advised we were to conduct ante mortem interviews on behalf of the Coroner. While we had reviewed this topic in our 2-day class, I never thought I would have to perform this function. After the briefing, I called the husband as promised. Due to the fact it was now approximately 8:00 p.m., I suggested meeting first thing the next morning. His reply was simply, "No, we want to meet you tonight." I replied I would come to their home and should arrive there by 9:00 p.m. During our conversation I explained the Coroner had asked that an ante mortem form be completed for each person on the aircraft. I shared with him we could complete the form on our visit or over the next several days. He said we could complete it when we met. I could hear over the phone several people in the background, as the noise level was somewhat loud. I suggested due to the sensitive nature of our conversation, he might only wish to have family members or a small number of people with him when we met. He said he would take care of it.

I told the command center leader I had agreed to meet with the family of the passenger once I arrived in ORD. I would need to have someone go with me since my CTM partner was not arriving until the next day. The Chicago command center leader became my CTM partner for the family meeting. I drove and she reviewed the ante mortem questions with me. (View sample ante mortem questions on page 36). We decided I would ask the ante mortem questions and she would record the responses. We would be slow, deliberate and patient. We would watch to see if we needed to take a break, but most importantly, we needed to be as compassionate and empathetic as possible.

We arrived at the family's house around 9:00 p.m. The husband answered the door, I introduced myself as well as my CTM partner, we shook hands and he led us to the dining room table to sit for our discussion. His brother and sister-in-law were also there. We offered our condolences and apologized having to meet under such difficult circumstances. I explained the role of CARE and the services we could provide. I explained we had been asked to complete the ante mortem questionnaire on behalf of the Coroner. I do not know how my CTM partner was feeling but I was nervous. My heart was beating fast and I was worried I would say the wrong thing. The family members were calm, somewhat quiet and willing to hear what we had to say. I am so grateful they were.

While preparing to begin the ante mortem questionnaire, the 10:00 p.m. news began. Naturally the crash of Flight 4184 was the lead story. Reports of the crash and short stories of several of the passengers and crew were shown, including a picture of the passenger we were assigned. My heart froze. Until then, I only knew her name. I did not know what she looked like but seeing her picture on television immediately made this real. The plane had crashed, people had died and I was sitting in the family dining room about to ask personal questions about someone I did not know from people who were stunned by the crash and their sudden loss.

Before the interview process began, we explained we would move at a pace the family was comfortable with. We would proceed as quickly or as slowly as they wished. We could take a break at any time and even come back the next day if we did not complete the interview in one sitting. There were eight or nine pages of questions. We proceeded at a very slow pace. As I asked the questions on the ante mortem form, my partner took notes of the answers given by the husband. I was surprised he had so much detailed information about his wife,

Flight 4184 Crash Sight

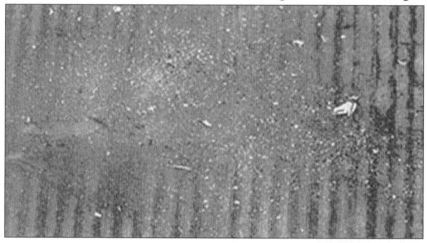

COURTESY OF THE: NTSB

such as her blood type in his day timer book. Someone ran upstairs to look at her shoes to determine the size. At one point the questions became even more personal with regards to female anatomy. I was uncomfortable asking those questions and simply turned to my CTM partner who must have noticed my hesitance because she instinctively took over the interview and I began to take the notes. Once those specific questions were completed, we switched places and I began to ask the questions again. I don't remember when this next comment was made, but I clearly remember, the sister-in-law saying, "Why are you asking these questions? Don't you even have a head to look at?" There was a long period of silence. I think we were all shocked by the question. I simply responded, "I'm very sorry to have to ask these sensitive questions. Every piece of information provided will help the Coroner in the positive identification of all those on board the aircraft." I thought it was very insensitive for her to ask such a graphic question considering this man had just lost his wife. No one in the room said a word. The silence was deafening. I remembered people display their emotions in different ways during a traumatic event. Everyone reacts differently. I also remembered our facilitators sharing with us listening may be the most important communication skill one may use. Often times, when you are searching for the right words to say it may be better to not say anything at all. Because I was comfortable with it, I found silence to be a very good friend. It was very challenging not to respond but it was the best thing to do. We completed the ante mortem interview, reviewed items and tasks we would be able to help the family with such as travel arrangements for out of town family members, hotel accommodations and, specifically, to share up to date information as we received it. We said we would be in contact with them the next morning to provide any new information received overnight. We thanked them for meeting with us at such a late hour, apologized again for meeting under such circumstances and left for the evening.

On the drive back to the command center we discussed how difficult and emotional the interview process was and how badly we felt for the family. I remember thinking, if something like this ever happened to my family; I hope I could be as calm as the husband was when we were talking with him. This was the only time I ever had to perform an ante mortem interview and I am very thankful I never had to do it again.

The next day, my new CTM partner arrived and I briefed her on the ante mortem interview performed the night before. We discussed how we would work with the family, who would ask the questions and provide information, and who would take notes. Our plan did not work quite the way we expected. Over the course of the next several weeks a natural routine of sorts would develop. Each day CARE Team members would sign-in when they arrived at the command center and when we went to visit the family we would sign-out with the address of where we were going. Signing in and out and advising our location was for security purposes. My CTM partner and I even developed a rhythm while working with the family of the passenger who died. I seemed to gravitate to the mother of the passenger and my CTM partner talked with the husband. One of us asked the questions while the other took notes. We both understood the need to be professional at all times. We also worked well together. There is no room for personality conflicts among team members especially in front of a survivor or a family member. We knew our work was about the family members impacted by the response. It is not about whether or not your teammate and you get along personally. As mentioned previously, we settled into a routine where we were contacting the family multiple times during the day when we had new information to

Flight 4184 Debris Field

AP Images

provide. It was critical to share information when we received it. Our goal was to make sure our family heard any new information from us before the media reported it. Trust me, that in itself was a challenge.

We also knew integrity was critical when communicating. There was so much misinformation in the media, which just added to the grief families were experiencing. We were direct, factual and delivered what we promised. If we advised the family we would call them at 4:00 p.m., we called them at 4:00 p.m. Often times, we would either call the family or drive to their home to provide the information. During the response, CARE Team members were asked to obtain the medical and dental records of the passenger from the family member. We called our passenger's husband and asked how he would like us to obtain those records. We suggested he could contact the dentist and physician's offices and pick up the records himself or we would call on his behalf. He preferred to call each of the doctor's and authorized the release of the documents to us. My CTM partner and I would later pick up the records and x-rays and deliver them to the Coroners office at the temporary morgue. This was in 1994 long before privacy laws and the Health Insurance Portability and Accountability Act (HIPAA) were legislated. Several days later, the Coroner requested DNA samples for each person on board the aircraft. We were provided with a list of preferred items for DNA samples. We went to the home of the passenger, spoke with her husband, and explained what the Coroner had requested. He provided us the samples and we drove them directly to the temporary morgue facility in Roselawn, Indiana.

Daily briefings for the CARE Team members were a fundamental part of our day. In order to stay informed and abreast of current information the team members would meet at their designated command center or dial in to a conference bridge line. There were multiple command centers and all of them shared the bridge line to report on the various questions and information being shared from headquarters and all the centers. Typically, we would meet in the morning and in the late afternoon. I do not remember the exact count of how many CARE Team members we had in Chicago but I do remember it was standing room only in the conference room we were using. If we had any questions, as a team member, we would write them down and forward it to our command center leader who would pose the question on the bridge line. If a team could not make it to the command center they could call in for the briefing. There were always many questions. We were always reminded in our briefings to only provide information to the family that was factual because speculating on unconfirmed reports or information did not benefit anyone.

Families of the crew and passengers were anxious to have their family member identified so they could have their loved-one buried or cremated. What a daunting task for the Coroner. In this accident, the airplane struck the ground nose-first while flying at approximately 400 miles per hour. The devastation and debris field was enormous. There were no intact bodies. The Coroner had to use the ante mortem information gathered, as well as the DNA samples provided by the families, in order to positively identify everyone on board the aircraft. Rather than release each crewmember or passenger as they were identified, the Coroner decided he would not release any of the remains until all had been identified. He provided the number of passengers and crewmembers positively identified on a daily basis and we would share the information with the families.

There were many questions as to why the Coroner chose this course of action. When our family asked us why he was going to wait for everyone to be identified, we said we did not know but would try to find out. The answer was simple. He did not know how long it would take to positively identify all the passengers and crew. He did not want one family to have the remains identified only to have the other families have to wait until further identifications had been made. At least that was what we were told. We shared this information with our family.

One day, while we were all waiting for the identifications to be made, I had gone back to my hotel room to unwind. My pager sounded and it was the funeral director calling. The husband was at the funeral home selecting a burial site for his wife. The funeral director wanted to know if American Eagle was going to pay for the site and also for the site for the husband. I was not sure how to respond. I knew we would pay for the passenger but did not know what the answer was about her husband so I asked for a few minutes to find out the answer to their question. I called the Chicago command center and asked. I was advised the airline would pay for the burial site of the passenger

Flight 4184

COURTESY OF THE : NTSB

that died but not for the husband. I provided this information to the funeral director. There was no pushback, no additional discussion. I learned then it was better to be comfortable saying, "I don't know but I will find out." It is impossible for team members to know the answer to every question. It was better not to make something up. Never lie or promise something you are not sure you can deliver.

While many of the families, including ours, decided to have a memorial service for their loved one before the identified remains were released. My CTM partner and I inquired of our family what we could do to help with the logistics and planning of the memorial. They were very gracious, very kind, but politely told us they would take care of it.

On the day of the Memorial, my CTM partner and I went to the location where the service would be held to ensure everything was set up appropriately. We were amazed at the number of flower arrangements, plants, and cards on display. Being somewhat curious, we walked around the large room, searching for the floral arrangement sent by the airline. After much searching, we found a very small plant on the floor with a card signed by American Eagle. We were shocked by the small size and personally offended at what had been sent. We were so embarrassed, for a brief moment we even considered changing the cards from one of the larger arrangements to our smaller one. Of course we didn't. The memorial service for our passenger was filled with fond memories, funny stories, laughter and tears. Over 800 people came to the service, with people standing in the hallways and even outside the building.

When the service was over, my CTM partner and I returned to the command center anxiously waiting to advise the command center leader about the offensiveness of the flower arrangement. Another family was having a memorial service the same evening in a different location. The team members for that service arrived back at the command center approximately the same time we did. We all had similar complaints about the size of the floral arrangement. We did some checking and discovered individuals responsible for ordering flowers had incorrectly determined the amount of money to spend on the arrangements based on AMR Rules and Regulations which were the company's guidelines for the overall operation of the company and behavior for employees. The guidelines provided, in the event of the death of an employee, the supervisor or manager should send the family a floral arrangement or plant valued at approximately $25. I shake my head as I write this to even think someone would believe a $25 arrangement, even in 1994, would be appropriate to send the family after a plane crash. This policy was immediately revised and a more appropriate floral arrangement, such as a wreath or spray of flowers, became the standard.

Until the crew and passengers were identified for interment, many memorial services were given in honor of those who died on Flight 4184. One was dedicated to the American Eagle crewmembers, another was for the emergency response providers and, of course, many families, as ours did, held their own private services for their loved one. I cried at every memorial. Not a blubbery sob, but tears for those who died and those who suffered a loss of a loved one. We would always be briefed before each memorial to turn off our pagers. We double-checked with each other before sitting down for the memorial to make sure the pager was off. There were at least eight nationalities on board Flight 4184 and, during one of the multi-faith services, someone's pager went off during the service. All of the CARE Team members were looking at each other to see who the guilty person was. The pager went off again, and then we all noticed a priest on the stage reaching for his pager. We all had a good laugh when we got on the busses back to the command center. We told our command center leader she should make sure the clergy and religious representatives also had their pagers off before the next memorial service. A little more than three weeks passed from the accident until the Coroner had positively identified everyone on board and the remains were released for burial.

My CTM partner and I asked the family for permission to attend the funeral and they graciously said yes. It was a lovely service, reflective and emotional. We were honored to have attended. After the service there was a wake at the home of the passenger's mother. My CTM partner and I wanted to bring something to the wake in remembrance of the passenger. We had been told previously she been very fond of Chinese food. We found a local Chinese restaurant and ordered egg rolls and fortune cookies and brought them to the home. I remember being in the kitchen with the mother, the passenger's sisters and brother and my CARE Team partner. The family had a custom of adding a particular saying at the end of the fortune inside the cookie. We opened our fortune cookies and read our fortunes with the added saying and laughed together as we read what was written on each tiny piece of paper.

The day my teammate and I ended our assignment we visited with the family one last time. We provided contact details on where they could call or write if they had questions or were looking for information they might need. We thanked them each for being so kind and gracious in allowing us the opportunity to serve them during such an emotional time. There were many tears shed on the day we left.

I will never forget the passenger's mother grabbing me by the shoulders. She was crying, as was I, and she said, "You go home and tell your mother I said she has a very special son." I could not believe what she had just said to me. Her daughter was dead and she was thanking me for being there for her and her family. I never expected to be thanked. I was humbled. I remember thinking I could not have been more blessed to have such kind and loving people to serve. I did go home and tell my mother how lucky she was and how much I loved her. I will never forget how reassuring and calm the family we worked with was during the initial days after the accident. It was a difficult situation for all of us but I am ever so thankful for the strength, the resilience and the courage the family displayed. A true testimony to the human spirit and how resilient people can be.

Several months later, my CARE Team partner and I were notified there were several personal belongings of our passenger which were ready to be returned to the next-of-kin, in this case, her husband. We were once again deployed to Chicago this time to return the personal belongings. I called the husband and set up a date and time to meet in person to return his wife's items. My CTM partner and I flew to Chicago and we reserved a meeting room in the American Airlines Admiral's Club at O'Hare Airport where we would meet the husband. We only had small box of items to give him. We did not know what was in the box but had heard very little survived the crash. He seemed disappointed we did not have more to give him than a few credit cards and an identification card, items that he showed us.

Our work was now complete. The deployment, which lasted just over three weeks, was over. Approximately 480 team member volunteers responded to the accident including reservation agents, management employees and CARE Team members. There were several logistical debriefs following the deployment to review lessons learned, what worked well and what did not work well. It was emotionally exhausting for all involved but nothing compared to the loss each family experienced.

Sometime in early 1995, before the one-year anniversary of the crash of Flight 4184, a news story reported approximately 18 caskets of unidentified remains from flight 4184 had been secretly buried without the families being notified. The news of this happening quickly spread from team member to team member. We were all horrified something like this could happen. The volunteers I talked with were all very angry as I was. We were furious. We could only imagine how angry the family members must have been when they learned of the secret burial. Many of the team members, myself included, felt betrayed by our corporate leadership. We felt like our personal integrity had been compromised. We volunteered for the response to 4184. We wanted to help those impacted by this awful crash. Now we learned of a secret burial. We did not know what to think. In August 1995, the families of Flight 4184 and the CARE Team members who responded, along with many others, were invited to a memorial dedication service at Calumet Cemetery in Merrillville, Indiana. The service was to pay respect to the unidentified remains of the 68 passengers and crew, which had been secretly buried.

The family members met at a central location at the cemetery and were transported by bus the short distance to the memorial site. The CARE Team members were staged behind where the families would sit. We would not be sitting with the families. As the families stepped off the bus, each looked for their CARE Team Member. I saw our family and my CTM partner and I went over to shake hands and hug each of them. We were so happy to see each other again. When the service was over, white roses were given to each family member to place on the memorial site. Our family asked us to walk with them to place their flowers on the memorial. Other families did the same thing. I cannot begin to describe how this made us feel. The continued support, compassion and empathy shown to us by the grieving family encouraged my CTM partner and me to continue this work. Other families also displayed similar support to their CARE Team members.

I will always remember the tragedy and sorrow of Flight 4184. I will also remember the resilient human spirit I was so lucky to experience. Twenty years later I still think about the kind words the mother told me when I left Chicago and I still carry the emotion of hearing them as if it were yesterday. While my goal in responding to our family affected by the crash of Flight 4184 was to make a difference in their lives, I was not prepared for the difference they made in mine. I am forever grateful.

Lessons Learned

There were so many lessons learned during the response to Flight 4184. It was the first major accident since the beginning of the CARE Program for AMR Corporation in 1993. I have included a few of these lessons for your consideration:

1 **Remember what your role is in your company's response.** Follow the established guidelines as prescribed. Do not deviate from your role.

2 **Only provide factual information.** Speculating on unconfirmed reports or information does not benefit anyone and reduces your credibility.

3 **Be professional at all times.** There is no room for personality conflicts among team members.

4 **Integrity is critical.** Say what you mean and deliver what you promise.

5 **Never promise something you are not capable of delivering.** If you do not have an answer to a question, be comfortable in saying "I do not know, but will find out and get back to you."

6 **Attend defusings and debriefings.** It is important to keep your emotions in check while responding.

7   **Talk to your own family before you leave on assignment.**
It is important they understand the type of service you will be
providing. You may not come back from assignment the same
person you were before you left.

8   **Be comfortable with silence.** Listening may be the best communication skill you use during a response. Be flexible. You may
be asked to perform various duties during your response.

9   **Exercise.** Take a walk. Get plenty of sleep. The more you can
work one of these into your schedule the better you will be able
to assist the family.

10   **Determine in advance a plan of action.** If two people are
responding as a team, determine who will ask questions and who
will take notes. Who will conduct the introductions and who will
recap with the family the actions to be taken.

Flight 4184

Executive Summary

On October 31, 1994, at 1559 Central Standard Time, an Avions de Transport Regional, model 72-212 (ATR 72), registration number N401AM, leased to and operated by Simmons Airlines, Incorporated, and doing business as American Eagle flight 4184, crashed during a rapid descent after an uncommanded roll excursion. The airplane was in a holding pattern and was descending to a newly assigned altitude of 8,000 feet when the initial roll excursion occurred. The airplane was destroyed by impact forces; and the captain, first officer, 2 flight attendants and 64 passengers received fatal injuries. Flight 4184 was a regularly scheduled passenger flight being conducted under 14 Code of Federal Regulations, Part 121; and an instrument flight rules flight plan had been filed.

The National Transportation Safety Board determines that the probable causes of this accident were the loss of control, attributed to a sudden and unexpected aileron hinge moment reversal that occurred after a ridge of ice accreted beyond the deice boots because: 1) ATR failed to completely disclose to operators, and incorporate in the ATR 72 airplane flight manual, flightcrew operating manual and flightcrew training programs, adequate information concerning previously known effects of freezing precipitation on the stability and control characteristics, autopilot and related operational procedures when the ATR 72 was operated in such conditions; 2) the French Directorate General for Civil Aviation's inadequate oversight of the ATR 42 and 72, and its failure to take the necessary corrective action to ensure continued airworthiness in icing conditions; and 3) the French Directorate General for Civil Aviation's failure to provide the Federal Aviation Administration with timely airworthiness information developed from previous ATR incidents and accidents in icing conditions, as specified under the Bilateral Airworthiness Agreement and Annex 8 of the International Civil Aviation Organization.

Contributing to the accident were: 1) the Federal Aviation Administration's failure to ensure that aircraft icing certification requirements, operational requirements for flight into icing conditions, and Federal Aviation Administration published aircraft icing information adequately accounted for the hazards that can result from flight in freezing rain and other icing conditions not specified in 14 Code of Federal Regulations, Part 25, Appendix C; and 2) the Federal Aviation Administration's inadequate oversight of the ATR 42 and 72 to ensure continued airworthiness in icing conditions.

Vii

Flight 4184

The safety issues in this report focused on communicating hazardous weather information to flightcrews, Federal regulations regarding aircraft icing and icing certification requirements, the monitoring of aircraft airworthiness, and flightcrew training for unusual events/attitudes.

Safety recommendations concerning these issues were addressed to the Federal Aviation Administration, the National Oceanic and Atmospheric Administration, and AMR Eagle. Also, as a result of this accident, on November 7, 1994, the Safety Board issued five safety recommendations to the Federal Aviation Administration regarding the flight characteristics and performance of ATR 42 and ATR 72 airplanes in icing conditions. In addition, on November 6, 1995, the Safety Board issued four safety recommendations to the Federal Aviation Administration concerning the Air Traffic Control System Command Center. In accordance with Annex 13 to the Convention on International Civil Aviation, the Bureau Enquetes-Accidents provided comments on the Safety Board's draft of the accident report that are contained in Volume II of this report.

Flight 4184

Executive Summary

General

The BEA strongly disagrees with substantial portions of the Factual, and with the Analysis, Conclusions, and Probable Cause sections of the report. In the BEA's view, except for the Recommendations section, the present report is incomplete, inaccurate, and unbalanced, It appears to have been influenced by an a priori belief on the probable cause of this accident The BEA strongly believes that today one-sided approach is detrimental to the cause of international aviation safety.

The Factual section selectively reports the facts of this accident. Some relevant facts are omitted and some other which are included are simply not accurate or their presentation is misleading. The BEA regrets it, since it had already advised the NTSB of a number of significant omissions, inaccuracies, and misrepresentations through his three sets of comments to the earlier drafts of this section, and since it was agreed that many of these errors would be rectified.

The Analysis and Conclusions sections are hampered by the incomplete and inaccurate Factual section. "Many of the issues which are discussed are addressed in an incorrect or incomplete manner. Those sections also regrettably omit any discussion of several highly relevant issues for safety and for the understanding of this accident and fail to address a true combination of factors which has caused it. They clearly are inconsistent with the safety recommendations which follow.

Given the facts of this accident, the current Probable Cause statement, which ignores critical causal factors, is unbalanced, not correct, and detrimental to the public concern for safety.

Accordingly, the BEA considers that the report requires substantial reworking. Acknowledging the necessity, for achieving true aviation safety to take into consideration all relevant aspects of the aviation system, outside any national consideration or any a priori sharing of blame or liability, it has expended significant efforts to prepare in these comments such a substantial reworking of all or part of the quoted sections, to assist the NTSB in making the necessary revision and facilitate the inclusion of the comments.

Flight 4184

National Transportation Safety Board
Washington, DC 20594

Brief of Accident

Adopted 10/22/1996

Printed on : 10/03/2014 03:38:46 PM

DCA95MA001
File No. 2070

10/31/1994   ROSELAWN, IN   Aircraft Reg No. N401AM   Time (Local): 15:59 CST

	Make/Model:	Atr/ATR-72-212
	Engine Make/Model:	P&W / 127
	Aircraft Damage:	Destroyed
	Number of Engines:	2
	Operating Certificate(s):	Flag Carrier/Domestic
	Name of Carrier	AMERICAN EAGLE AIRLINES
	Type of Flight Operation:	Scheduled; Domestic; Passenger Only
	Reg. Flight Conducted Under:	Part 121: Air Carrier

		Fatal	Serious	Minor/None
	Crew	4	0	0
	Pass	64	0	0

Last Depart. Point: INDIANAPOLIS, IN
Destination: CHICAGO, IL
Airport Proximity: Off Airport/Airstrip

Condition of Light: Dusk
Weather Info Src: Unknown
Basic Weather: Instrument Conditions
Lowest Ceiling: 500 Ft. AGL, Overcast
Visibility: 0.50 SM
Wind Dir/Speed:
Temperature (°C): 4
Precip/Obscuration:

Pilot-in-Command   Age: 29

Certificate(s)/Rating(s)
Airline Transport; Flight Instructor. Commercial; Multi-engine Land; Single-engine Land

Instrument Ratings
Airplane

Flight Time (Hours)

Total All Aircraft: 7867
Last 90 Days: 190
Total Make/Model: 1548
Total Instrument Time: Unk/Nr

*** Note: NTSB investigators traveled in support of this investigation and used data obtained from various sources to prepare this aircraft accident report. ***

The airplane was in a holding pattern and was descending to a newly assigned altitude of 8,000 feet when it experienced an uncommanded roll excursion and crashed during a rapid descent. The loss of control was attributed to a sudden and unexpected aileron hinge moment reversal that occurred after a ridge of ice accreted beyond the deice boots. The manufacturer failed to disseminate adequate warnings and guidance to operators about the adverse characteristics of, and techniques to recover from, ice-induced aileron hinge moment reversal events; to failed to develop additional airplane modifications, which led directly to this accident. The DGAC failed to require the manufacturer to take additional corrective actions, such as performing additional icing tests, issuing more specific warnings regarding the aileron hinge moment reversal phenomenon, developing additional airplane modifications, and providing specific guidance on the recovery from a hinge moment reversal, which led directly to this accident. The ability of the FAA to monitor, on a real-time basis, the continued airworthiness of the ATR airplanes was hampered by the inadequately defined lines of communication, the inadequate means for the FAA to retrieve pertinent information, and the DGAC's failure to provide the FAA with critical airworthiness information, because of the DGAC's apparent belief that the information was not required to be provided under the terms of the Bilateral Airworthiness Agreement.

VIP INTERVIEW FORMS

DMORT Family Assistance Team

Antemortem Interview Forms

- For official use only -

EXAMPLE: Ante Mortem Interview (Page 1 of 9)

Flight 4184

VIP Personal Information
Page 1 of 8   Morgue Reference No. _____

NDMS·USA DMORT

RM #

Name	/	/	/			If Female/Maiden Name	
	Last	Suffix	First	Middle	Sex		Age

DOB	Race	Social Security # / Other	Birth City	State/Country	Birth Hospital

Address | | Apt # | City | | State | Zip

County | | Country | USA | Inside City Limits | | Religious Preference

Education: level completed. Elem/Second (0-12): | | College | | Degree Earned:

Alias 1 | | Alias 2 |
      Last   First   Middle   Last   First   Middle

Phone (H) | Phone (W) | Phone (Cell)

Marital Status   ○ Married   ○ Never Married   ○ Widowed   ○ Divorced   ○ Separated   ○ Unknown   **Wedding Date**

Spouse | | | | | ○ Living ○ Deceased ○ Unknown
     Last   Suffix   Maiden/birth Name   First   Middle

Father | | | | ○ Living ○ Deceased ○ Unknown
     Last   Suffix   First   Middle

Mother | | | | ○ Living ○ Deceased ○ Unknown
     Last   Maiden/birth Name   First   Middle

Legal Next Of Kin | | | **Home**
     Last   First   Middle
Address | | **Work**
City | **State** | **Zip** | **On Site/Cell Phone**
Relationship: ○ Wife ○ Husband ○ Father ○ Mother ○ Brother ○ Sister ○ Son ○ Daughter ○ Uncle ○ Aunt ○ Other
Permenant Contact | Please place name and contact info here   **Other:**

Informant

	/	/			Relationship
Last	Suffix	First	Middle		○ Wife ○ Daughter
Address		Zip	City	State	○ Husband ○ Uncle
Home Phone	Work Phone	Cell Phone	email		○ Father ○ Cousin
Date of Initial Contact		Type of Initial Contact			○ Mother ○ Employer
					○ Brother ○ Friend
					○ Sister ○ Other
					○ Son

Contacts

	/	/			Relationship
Last	Suffix	First	Middle		○ Wife ○ Daughter
Address		Zip	City	State	○ Husband ○ Uncle
Home Phone	Work Phone	Cell Phone	email		○ Father ○ Aunt
Date of Initial Contact		Type of Initial Contact			○ Mother ○ Cousin
					○ Brother ○ Employer
					○ Sister ○ Friend
					○ Son ○ Other

EXAMPLE: Ante Mortem Interview (Page 2 of 9)

Flight 4184

VIP Physical Description

Page 2 of 8   Morgue Reference No. _____

RM # _____

Name ___/___/_____/___

Last	Suffix	First	Initial	Age	DOB	Sex	Race

Height Inches: | Height cm   **Approx. Weight (Pounds):** | Weight Kilos

Hair Info

Hair Color
- ☐ Auburn ☐ Brown ☐ Gray ☐ Salt & Pepper ☐ Other
- ☐ Blonde ☐ Black ☐ Red ☐ White

Please place other here

Hair Length
- ○ Bald ○ Short < 3" ○ Male Patern Baldness: *Description*
- ○ Shaved ○ Medium ○ Long

Hair Accessory ☐ Extensions ☐ Hair Piece ☐ Hair Transplant ☐ Wig ☐ N/A

Hair Description ○ Curly ○ Wavy ○ Straight ○ N/A ○ Other:

Facial Hair Type
- ○ Clean Shaven ○ Beard & Moustache ○ Goatee ○ Sideburns ○ N/A
- ○ Moustache ○ Beard ○ Stubble ○ Lower Lip

Facial Hair Color
- ○ Blonde ○ Black ○ Red ○ White   **Facial Hair Notes:**
- ○ Brown ○ Gray ○ Salt & Pepper ○ NA

Eyes

Eye Color ○ Blue ○ Brown ○ Green ○ Hazel ○ Gray ○ Black ○ Other:

Optical Color/Descrip: _____

Optical Lens ☐ Contacts ☐ Glasses ☐ Implants ☐ None   **Desc.**

Eye Status ☐ Both Intact ☐ Missing R ☐ Missing L ☐ Glass R ☐ Glass L ☐ Catarac

Nails

Fingernail Type ○ Natural ○ Artificial ○ Unknown   **Length** ○ Extremely Long ○ Long ○ Medium ○ Short

Fingernail Color _____   **Description**

Characteristics ☐ Bitten ☐ Decorated ☐ Misshapen ☐ Yellowed/Fungus ☐ N/A

Toenail Color _____   **Toenail description**

Characteristics ☐ Decorated ☐ Misshapen ☐ Yellowed/Fungus ☐ N/A

Body Piercing(s)? ○ Yes ○ No   **Photos?** ○ Yes ○ No   **Photo Location** _____

#	Location	Side	Quantity	Description (include evidence of old piercings)	Photo
1					
2					
3					

Tattoo(s) ○ Yes ○ No   **Photos?** ○ Yes ○ No   **Photo Location**

#	Location	Side	Tattoo Description
1			
2			
3			
4			

EXAMPLE: Ante Mortem Interview (Page 3 of 9)

Flight 4184

VIP Medical History
Page 3 of 8

Morgue Reference No. _____

Name _____ / __ / _____ / __

| Last | Suffix | First | Middle | Age | DOB | Sex | Race |

DENTIST

Dentist _____ Last _____ First _____ ○ Dental Info Listed ○ Unknown ○ Never

Address _____ Zip _____ City _____ State _____

Phone 1 _____ Phone 2 _____

See Dental Section For Additional Dental Information

Dental Records Received ○ Yes ○ No

☐ Dental Work
☐ Dentures
☐ Both
☐ Braces
☐ Partials
☐ Tooth Jewelry

Additional Dental Information/2nd Dentist: _____

PHYSICIAN

Physician _____ Last _____ First _____

Address _____

Zip _____ City _____ State _____

Phone 1 _____ Phone 2 _____

Email _____

Practice Name _____

Physician Type _____

Reason Seen: _____

Records Requested ○ Yes ○ No

Records Obtained ○ Yes ○ No

PHYSICIAN

Physician _____ Last _____ First _____

Address _____

Zip _____ City _____ State _____

Phone 1 _____ Phone 2 _____

Email _____

Practice Name _____

Physician Type _____

Reason Seen: _____

Records Requested ○ Yes ○ No

Records Obtained ○ Yes ○ No

Medical Radiographs? ○ Yes ○ No ○ Unknown

Medical Radiographs Location: _____

Potential Type of Radiographs - and dates taken if known:

_____
_____
_____

Old Fractures: Description: _____

○ Yes ○ No

Objects in Body: ☐ Pacemaker ☐ Bullets ☐ Implants ☐ Needles ☐ Shrapnel ☐ Other _____

Surgery: ☐ Gall Bladder ☐ Tracheotomy ☐ Caesarean ☐ Reconstructive ☐ Other _____
☐ Appendectomy ☐ Laparotomy ☐ Mastectomy ☐ Open heart

Diabetic? ☐ Yes ☐ No ☐ Unknown   If Female / pregnancy in the past 12 months ? ☐ Yes ☐ No ☐ Unknown

Unique Characteristics   **Description of: Scars, Operations, birthmarks, burns, missing organs, amputations, other special characteristics :**

○ Yes ○ No
_____
_____
_____
_____

Prosthetic Location/Description

Prosthetic(s)
_____
○ Yes ○ No

EXAMPLE: Ante Mortem Interview (Page 4 of 9)

Flight 4184

VIP Personal Information
Page 4 of 8   Morgue Reference No. _____

RM # _____

Name _____ / _____ / _____ /

| Last | Suffix | First | Initial | Age | DOB | Sex | Race |

Group Status: ◯ Alone ◯ Group **Group Type:** _____ **Fam/Grp Name:** _____

Date last seen: _____ Family, Sports, Church, Military, etc.

Last seen with: _____

Last location Victim was seen: _____

Military Service: _____ **Branch:** _____ **Country** _____ **Service Number** _____

Approximate Service Date _____ **Military DNA Taken:** ◯ Yes ◯ No ◯ Unknown

Immigration Status: _____ **Resident Alien Card (Green Card)** ◯ Yes ◯ No **Ever Finger Printed:** _____

☐ Fingerprints ☐ Footprints **Prints Located:** _____

Ever been Arrested: _____ **Arrested By:** _____ **Ever in Prison or Jail:** _____

Prison or Jail Location: _____

Usual Occupation: _____ **Type of Business or Industry:** _____

Employer: _____ **Employer Phone:** _____

Employer Address: _____

List memberships: Clubs, Fraternities, etc.

Additional Data:

EXAMPLE: Ante Mortem Interview (Page 5 of 9)

Flight 4184

VIP Jewelry
Page 5 of 8

Morgue Reference No. _____

RM #

Name	/	/		/					
Last		Suffix	First		Initial	Age	DOB	Sex	Race

WATCH:

#	Type/ Make	Band Material Watch Face Color	Description	Photo Available Inscription
1				Yes No
2				Yes No

JEWELRY:

#	Jewelry/Type Style	Material Color/	Size / Where Worn/ Frequently Worn?	Description	Photo Available Inscription
1			Yes No		Yes No
2			Yes No		Yes No
3			Yes No		Yes No
4			Yes No		Yes No
5			Yes No		Yes No
6			Yes No		Yes No
7			Yes No		Yes No

Other Commonly Carried Personal Effects _____

_____

_____

Cell Phone ○ Yes ○ No ○ Unknown   **Cell Phone Type:** _____   **Service Provider:** _____

Cell Phone Number _____   **Cell Phone Description** _____

EXAMPLE: Ante Mortem Interview (Page 6 of 9)

Flight 4184

VIP Clothing and Personal Effects
Page 6 of 8   Morgue Reference No. _____

RM #

Name

	/	/			/				
Last		Suffix		First		Initial	Age	DOB	Sex	Race

#	Clothing Items	Color	Description	Size
1				
2				
3				
4				
5				
6				
7				
8				
9				
10				
11				
12				
13				
14				

CLOTHING:

Wallet: Description _____
Contents _____

Purse: Description _____
Contents _____

Pockets: Contents Left _____

Contents Right _____

EXAMPLE: Ante Mortem Interview (Page 7 of 9)

Flight 4184

Morgue Reference No. _____

RM # ____

Name ____ / ____ / ____ / ____

Last	Suffix	First	Initial	Age	DOB	Sex	Race

Potential Living Biological Donors
All BIOLOGICAL Relatives of Missing Individual
Such as: Mother/Father/Spouse/Sister/Brother/Children/Uncle/Aunt/Cousin

➕ Add New Donor

Last Name	First Name	Middle Name	Email	DOB	Sex
Relationship	Address	Zip	City	State	Phone 1	Phone 2

Last Name	First Name	Middle Name	Email	DOB	Sex
Relationship	Address	Zip	City	State	Phone 1	Phone 2

Last Name	First Name	Middle Name	Email	DOB	Sex
Relationship	Address	Zip	City	State	Phone 1	Phone 2

Last Name	First Name	Middle Name	Email	DOB	Sex
Relationship	Address	Zip	City	State	Phone 1	Phone 2

Last Name	First Name	Middle Name	Email	DOB	Sex
Relationship	Address	Zip	City	State	Phone 1	Phone 2

Last Name	First Name	Middle Name	Email	DOB	Sex
Relationship	Address	Zip	City	State	Phone 1	Phone 2

Last Name	First Name	Middle Name	Email	DOB	Sex
Relationship	Address	Zip	City	State	Phone 1	Phone 2

Last Name	First Name	Middle Name	Email	DOB	Sex
Relationship	Address	Zip	City	State	Phone 1	Phone 2

Primary donor for Nuclear DNA Analysis

An "appropriate family member" for nuclear DNA Analysis is someone that is biologically related to and only one generation removed from the deceased. The following are the family members who are appropriate donors to provide reference specimens, and in the order of preference (family members highlighted in bold print are the most desirable):

1. Natural (Biological) **Mother and Father**, AND   2. **Spouse** and Natural (Biological) **Children**, AND
3. A Natural (Biological) Mother or Father and victim's biological children, OR
4. Multiple Full Siblings of the Victim (i.e., children from the same Mother and Father)

EXAMPLE: Ante Mortem Interview (Page 8 of 9)

Flight 4184

VIP Interviewer Information

RM #

Morgue Reference No. _____

Deceased Name _____ / ___ / _____ / _____
Last   Suffix   First   Middle

Interview Location _____   Date _____   Time _____
(MM/DD/YYYY)

Interviewer Info:

    Interviewer Name _____
       Full Name

    Interviewing Organization _____

Interviewer Home Information

    Address: _____

    Home phone: _____

    Cell Phone: _____

    Work Phone: _____

Interviewer Onsite Information

    Interviewer Onsite address: _____
       Location Name and Street,City, State and Room #

    Interviewer Onsite phone: _____

    Interviewer Onsite cell: _____

Reviewer Info

    Reviewer Name: _____

    Reviewer Signature: _____

    Reviewing agency: _____

EXAMPLE: Ante Mortem Interview (Page 9 of 9)

Flagship Airlines 3379
D.B.A. American Eagle

Raleigh-Durham, North Carolina

December 13, 1994

O N DECEMBER 13, 1994, AROUND 2:00 p.m., several CARE Team members and I were at DFW airport attending an employee assistance critical incident stress debriefing (CISD) facilitated by the company's Employee Assistance Program (EAP). American Airlines provided ongoing voluntary debriefs in the aftermath of responding to the crash of American Eagle of Flight 4184. There were only a handful of volunteers attending this session yet many of us had similar things on our mind. One or two people were having dreams of another crash, others were having difficulty sleeping and I was having challenges settling back into my home and work routine. The person facilitating our session told us the feelings and emotions we were experiencing were normal after the type of work we had just completed. I'm sure there were other things said but overall I left feeling a little better knowing other volunteers were experiencing similar emotions. Our session ended around 3:00 p.m. and I went back to headquarters to finish the workday.

After work I went Christmas shopping with a friend. Only eleven days until Christmas Eve. I was driving home listening to music on the radio when it was time for a scheduled news update. There was a report of an American Eagle crash in Raleigh-Durham, North Carolina. My heart sank; I could not believe what I was hearing. The same news channel, the same drive home as with 4184 and it was all happening again. My mind immediately went back to the afternoon CISD. People were having dreams of another accident and now there was one. How could this happen so soon after flight 4184? Shortly after arriving home, I received a call from the CARE command center to check my availability for deployment. I was told Flight 3379 crashed with 20 passengers and crew on board. We knew there were fatalities but did not yet know how many. I confirmed my availability and was asked to report to the American Airlines Southern Reservations Office (SRO). The SRO is where the largest reservation center for AA is located and where families would call for information regarding the accident.

After arriving at the SRO I was briefed along with the other volunteer team members. Several of us, including myself, had begun our career in the reservations department. We would be taking phone calls from people who believed they had a loved one on the flight. We were to gather as much information as possible from the caller including information such as name, phone number, address, and relationship to the passenger. We would use this information to help us verify who was an actual family member versus someone from the media or a person just curious about the accident. While a number of us were taking calls, another group was verifying the passenger manifest.

I do not know how many calls I made or received that evening but I do remember one in particular. I made a phone call to a woman who had called in to the reservation center. She was inquiring about her son and his wife. When I called her back she began to yell at me for

American Airlines flying the same type of aircraft as had crashed just a few months earlier in Indiana. I started to explain it was a different aircraft when I suddenly realized it didn't matter what kind of plane it was. I was patient and just listened. I knew this was not personal. As I mentioned in Chapter 2 with Flight 4184, an aviation disaster is a very emotional event. The people you work with whether a survivor, family member or another team member may not always be kind to you. Remember, their response may be more about the emotion than it is about you personally. I waited until the woman finished talking and apologized to her for the accident and having to go through this. I gathered the information I had been taught to collect and confirmed they were on the flight. However, I advised we did not have any information regarding their condition at that time as we were still trying to determine if there were survivors and, if so, which hospital had they been taken to. She quickly stopped me and told me she knew her son was alive because she had talked to him. I asked if I could place her on hold for a moment and then I collected my thoughts. I went back to the call and asked what hospital her son had been taken to and advised I would do what I could to find out information regarding her daughter-in-law. I also asked if she had the name of the next-of-kin for her daughter-in-law aside from her husband. She provided me with the name of the mother of the female passenger and her phone number.

Once I was off the phone line I contacted one of the command center leaders and shared what I had just learned. We began researching what information we had regarding each of the passengers. It appeared, while there were survivors, they had been taken to various hospitals. I had promised to call the woman who was the mother of the male passenger every hour on the hour whether I had new information or not. One of the command center leaders continued to research where the female passenger may have been taken and I continued to

Flight 3379 Debris Field

COURTESY OF THE: NTSB

take inbound calls from other concerned family and friends. I also contacted the mother of the female passenger, advised her who I was and I would be her contact for information. I also promised her I would call her every hour whether I had any new information or not.

It was several hours before I would learn what had happened to the young woman who was traveling with her husband on Flight 3379. While he had survived the accident she had died as a result of her injuries. As the confirmation of deaths occurred, those of us who had spoken with family members of the deceased were briefed on how to make a death notification phone call. Of the 20 passengers and crew on Flight 3379, there were only five survivors. We were asked if we were okay with making the call or would we prefer someone else to do it. I believe we all made the necessary phone call.

Before I made the call to the mother to advise her that her daughter had died, I removed my headset and left the room. I grabbed something to drink, water or soft drink, and walked around the floor of the building. I could not believe this was happening again. I was dazed and feeling anxious about making the call. I went back to my position and leaned closely into the computer because I just wanted to hide from everyone, I nervously dialed the number. When the mother answered the phone I introduced myself as if we had never talked over the past several hours. I advised her there had been an accident and she stopped me and said, "Just tell me the news." I told her daughter had died as a result of her injuries from the crash and she screamed, started to cry and dropped the phone. A few seconds later someone else picked up the phone and asked what I had just said to make the mother so upset. I asked who I was speaking with and was told she was a neighbor. I advised her of the death of the passenger and then she dropped the phone. A third person, a young man, picked up the phone and I asked him who he was. He said he was the brother of the passenger. I asked him how old he was because he sounded very young. I believe he was in his mid-teens. I also had noticed I could no longer hear the mother of the passenger crying in the background. I asked him where he was and why it had gotten so quiet. He shared with me he was standing in the kitchen pantry with the door closed so he could hear me. I asked him to get a piece of paper and something to write with so he could write down my contact details. I shared with him what I could regarding the message I had delivered. I do not remember if I told him his sister had died or if I had just delivered difficult news to his mother. I explained to him I would call back in a short time so he and his mom could talk about the phone call. After we disconnected I called the family of the husband of the passenger and provided the same news. It was a very long and emotional night.

There were no new volunteers for CARE. The volunteers who had just responded to flight 4184 in October were now being asked to redeploy for this accident. My CTM partner from the previous response and I were reconnected and asked to work with the families of the husband and wife I had spoken to the evening of the crash. There were already CARE Team members in Raleigh-Durham who would be assigned to the husband in the hospital and the team members would reach out to him while he was there. My CTM partner and I were asked to fly and meet with the family of his wife. I contacted the mother again and advised her we would be flying to her location the next day to meet with her. I offered my condolences and said I would contact her when we arrived.

As our family was the only family from this location, there was no command center just the two of us working out of our hotel rooms and listening to periodic updates via conference call. We were able to call the HDQ command center with any questions we had or for them to assist us with any thing we needed. We contacted the mother of the passenger, set up a time to meet and, proceeded to outline how we would conduct our meeting with her. We knew having a plan would help us stay focused, not to mention, reduce our anxiety some. In addition, it ensured we covered all the items we needed to. I personally believe the people we work with are put more at ease because being organized allows us to focus more on the individual and what they are experiencing. Once again, my partner and I decided I would ask the questions and she would take notes.

I drove to the home, knocked on the door, showed identification and we both hugged the mother. She invited us into the house and we began to explain our role. We shared with her our condolences and heartfelt sorrow for the loss of her daughter. We explained we could assist her with travel arrangements for family members, hotel accommodations and would be taking care of necessary expenses regarding the funeral and other immediate needs. My CTM partner was taking notes so as to not miss anything. When I was finished asking questions, my partner summarized the tasks we were to follow-up on. We agreed on a time we would call and provide an update with new information and the progress of the actions we had taken.

As we stood up to leave, the mother of the passengers said there was one thing she would like to do. She would like to talk to the young man that had called her about her daughter's death. She said it must have been the most difficult phone call he had ever made but at one point she just wanted to slap him. She began to laugh and said he must have been nervous because he had started the call by summarizing everything that was said on previous calls. My partner was smiling because she knew I was the one who called the mother. I was not going to tell her I had been the one to call her. The mother noticed my partner smiling and asked why she was smiling. My partner looked at me, I looked at her and then I looked at the mother. I said, "It was me who called you the night of the accident." She stepped forward to hug me but I thought she was going to slap me so I took a step back. We both laughed and then hugged and cried together. Somewhere deep inside me I was feeling a warmth of amazement about our encounter. This mother had just lost her daughter and she wanted to thank the person who called her the night of the accident. I was overwhelmed by her gratitude. It was so unexpected. That afternoon I began to realize human beings are very resilient, caring and forgiving when treated with compassion, empathy and respect.

My CTM partner and I went back to our hotel and began working on several requests of the family. We also discussed how our interaction with the mother went. We reviewed our conversation, discussed using the word "we" rather than "I" since we were a team. This was important to us because we wanted to convey to the family we were a team responding for them. In addition, we were talking with the team members, assisting the injured husband while he was in the hospital in Raleigh-Durham. We learned he would be released from the hospital in a few days and was in need of transportation home to the northeast. The passenger's family had shared with us he did not want to fly because his injuries would have made it challenging. Working with the HDQ command center, they were able to arrange a large van, equipped with a driver, a nurse, the passenger's mother and a comfortable area for the passenger to lie down while on the way home. The team members assigned to him would remain in Raleigh-Durham and my CTM partner and I would work with him and his family when he arrived home.

We continued to work with the mother of the young woman who died by providing updates regarding the accident investigation, travel arrangements for family arriving in town for the funeral, as well as visiting with the funeral home to ensure all the arrangements were paid for by the airline. As with the previous accident my CTM partner and I were continually briefed on what was happening at the Raleigh-Durham airport. We could call in to the conference bridge line two to three times a day to receive information we would share with the families we were assigned to. The identification process of the passengers and crew who died would not be as challenging as it had been with American Eagle Flight 4184. Actually, the remains of the deceased would be identified and returned home for burial in a matter of days. The aircraft, while in several pieces, was more intact than Flight 4184 was.

Almost every day I would check in with my manager from the Human Resources Department where I worked to advise her as to how things were going. I had not been in the office much for almost seven weeks due to responding to the two accidents. After visiting with the families one afternoon I came back to the hotel to find a package had arrived for me. It was from my colleagues in the department I worked in at headquarters. They had sent me a picture of my dogs, which had been on my desk, game books, candy and a card that everyone had signed. I was so grateful for their gift. My CTM partner and I had felt disconnected from our families and work and this gift of thoughtfulness was just what I needed.

The weather in the northeast was very cold. It was only a few days before Christmas and the surviving passenger was on his way home. We kept in contact by phone with his mother who was traveling with him to see how the drive was going and also to determine when they would arrive home. We had requested a nurse to arrive at the home shortly after the expected arrival time of the van which was sometime between 9:00 p.m. and 10:00 p.m. My CTM partner was going to the airport to pick up a family member and I was assigned a temporary CARE Team Member to go with me to meet the survivor and his family when they arrived to the house. Driving through the neighborhood to the house was very surreal. It was bitterly cold. Houses were decorated with Christmas lights and outside decorations. To be visiting someone we had not met who had survived a plane crash days before Christmas was surreal. My temporary CARE Team Member partner and I arrived at the house, walked up to the door and knocked. We were both wearing suits and winter coats. No one answered the door. After we had waited a few minutes, a neighbor walked over to see who we were. I can only imagine what he must have been thinking as two men in trench coats were knocking on his neighbors door late in the evening. We introduced ourselves and provided our company identification. He was very concerned about the family and knew they would be arriving soon. As we were talking, the van pulled up to the house and all of us proceeded to help the passenger and his mother move from the van into the house. Once everyone was settled in the home, we explained a home nurse would be arriving soon and there would be 24-hour care provided. We reviewed the services we would provide and asked what questions they may have. We shared we would be available 24/7 to answer their questions. Once the local nurse arrived and relieved the nurse from Raleigh-Durham, we said our goodbyes for the evening and returned to our hotel.

Over the next several days we assisted various family members from each of the passengers. We met with the funeral home director and provided an address where the funeral invoice should be sent. We purchased incidental items for the family members who flew in for the funeral. In addition, we coordinated immediate, on-going care for the survivor to attend to his medical needs. A few days after our arrival and our assistance began, the body of his wife arrived at the funeral home for burial. I remember visiting the mother of the deceased shortly after this and it appeared to me she was a little uneasy during our conversation. My CTM partner and I listened carefully to what she had to say and then I asked her if something was on her mind. She asked if it would be possible to get a floral wreath for her daughter's funeral. We both reassured her it was more than possible. I asked if she had a florist she would like to use and she provided us the name and telephone number of the florist. We made arrangements for the mother to order what she wanted and for the invoice to be sent to American Eagle for payment. The entire conversation reminded me about how important it is to pay attention to body language of people. Sometimes it is not the words people say, as it is their body language, or tone of voice that conveys the message.

On the day of the funeral the weather was gray with drizzling rain. The funeral service was performed at a local church. Across the street was a small shopping center with parking allowed on the side of the street. This would prove important later on. The funeral service was very nice and there were many, many people attending. When the service was over and the family walked out of the church, news reporters were across the street with their cameras filming everything. As all the people left the church, they could see the media frenzy on the street. My CTM partner and I were trying to figure out what we could do to stop this from happening but we did not have to. The family members and their friends formed a large semicircle in front of the media, shielding the immediate family from the cameras. It was amazing to see how everyone rallied around the family to support them during this difficult and challenging time.

A day or two after the funeral service, my CTM partner and I met with each of the families one last time. We provided them with phone contacts and addresses of how to stay in touch with American Eagle if they had additional questions or needs. We advised them someone from the airline would reach out to them in several days. We thanked each of the family members for allowing us the opportunity to serve them during this difficult time. Once again, tears were shed, hugs were given and we flew home.

AMR was very good giving time off for the volunteers and, coupled with vacation time I had remaining, I had about two weeks off from work. However, hard as I tried to get into the Christmas spirit, I just couldn't. I honestly do not remember Christmas with my family that year. I was too exhausted and emotionally spent after one and a half months of being away from home. All I could think about was how the families were coping with this being their first Christmas without their loved ones. I could not wait for the holidays to be over.

When I returned to work shortly after the beginning of the year, I thanked all my colleagues in the department I worked with for their support. It meant the world to me to know they not only cared about how I was doing but also respected the work all the volunteers were performing. Not all the responders received the support I did. I considered myself very lucky.

A couple of weeks after I was back at work, my manager called me to her office. She asked me how I was doing. I told her it was hard being back at work. My normal work did not seem as important as the work I had performed the past several months. She was concerned about me and even asked where my sense of humor had gone. I honestly could not answer her. I was tired, numb but did not know what to do. During the ongoing critical incident stress debriefs the airline held for us, I learned this was normal and, over time, things would get better. They did get better, I did get my sense of humor back, at least I thought so, and work became important again. However, I was a changed person. My life priorities shifted. While work had always been a focal point for me, my family was more important, my friends were important and helping the families in the aftermath of an air disaster was important. I had responded to two accidents back-to-back. Many team members had done this now. I hoped I would be as resilient as the families I had the honor to work with had been. I remember thinking, many people live a lifetime trying to make a difference in the world, I felt lucky, I already had.

Lessons Learned

Flight 3379 crashed almost six weeks after Flight 4184. There was no time for new procedures or enhancements to existing procedures. From a CARE Team member's perspective, many of the lessons learned from this flight are similar to those learned in 4184.

1 **Create an agenda.** Outline the main topics you want to review with the survivor/family member before you meet them. Having a plan keeps you organized and helps the family see you are prepared.

2 **Listen and watch.** Do not interrupt the survivor/family member. Often times it is not the words being said as it is the tone of voice or posture of the person speaking that conveys a message.

3 **Explain why you are taking notes.** Share with the family you are taking notes so you do not forget any task you need to perform or so you do not forget to answer any questions they may have. Better to write it down than to try and remember later.

4 **Review everything.** Review how you and your partner are working together. Use the term "we" instead of "I" when working with the family. Family assistance is a team approach.

5 **Be patient.** Responding to an aviation disaster is an emotional experience for everyone involved. Sometimes you have to let the emotion run its course until any action may be taken.

6 **Do not take things personally.** The people you work with whether it is a survivor, family member or other volunteer may not always be kind to you. Remember, in most cases, their response may be more about emotion than it is about you.

Flight 3379

Executive Summary

On December 13, 1994, at 1834, American Eagle (AMR) flight 3379 crashed about 4 nautical miles southwest of the runway 5L threshold during an instrument landing system approach to the Raleigh-Durham International Airport. Thirteen passengers and the two crewmembers were fatally injured, and the other five passengers survived. The airplane was destroyed by impact and fire. The weather at the time of the accident was ceiling 500 feet, visibility 2 miles, light rain and fog, temperature 38° F, and dew point 36° F. This was a regularly scheduled passenger flight under 1 4 Code of Federal Regulations, Part 135.

The National Transportation Safety Board determines that the probable causes of this accident were: 1) the captain's improper assumption that an engine had failed, and 2) the captain's subsequent failure to follow approved procedures for engine failure, single-engine approach and go-around, and stall recovery. Contributing to the cause of the accident was the failure of AMR Eagle/Flagship management to identify, document, monitor, and remedy deficiencies in pilot performance and training.

Safety issues examined in this report include flightcrew decisions and training, air carrier organization, hiring and recordkeeping practices, Federal Aviation Administration surveillance of AMR Eagle/Flagship, and the flight profile advisory system. Safety recommendations concerning these issues were made to the Federal Aviation Administration .

Flight 3379

National Transportation Safety Board
Washington, DC 20594

Brief of Accident

Adopted 06/22/1996

Printed on : 10/03/2014 03:51:52 PM

DCA95MA006
File No. 1771

12/13/1994   MORRISVILLE, NC   Aircraft Reg No. N918AE   Time (Local): 18:34 EST

Make/Model: British Aerospace/JETSTREAM 3201
Engine Make/Model: Garrett / TPE-331-12UHR
Aircraft Damage: Destroyed
Number of Engines: 2
Operating Certificate(s): Commuter Air Carrier; Flag Carrier/Domestic
Name of Carrier FLAGSHIP AIRLINES INC
Type of Flight Operation: Scheduled; Domestic; Passenger Only
Reg. Flight Conducted Under: Part 135: Air Taxi & Commuter

	Fatal	Serious	Minor/None
Crew	2	0	0
Pass	13	5	0

Last Depart. Point: GREENSBORO, NC
Destination: RALEIGH, NC
Airport Proximity: Off Airport/Airstrip

Condition of Light: Night/Dark
Weather Info Src: Weather Observation Facility
Basic Weather: Instrument Conditions
Lowest Ceiling: 500 Ft. AGL, Overcast
Visibility: 2.00 SM
Wind Dir/Speed: 010 / 008 kts
Temperature (°C): 3
Precip/Obscuration:

Pilot-in-Command   Age: 29

Certificate(s)/Rating(s)
Airline Transport; Commercial; Multi-engine Land; Single-engine Land

Instrument Ratings
Airplane

Flight Time (Hours)

Total All Aircraft: 3499
Last 90 Days: Unk/Nr
Total Make/Model: Unk/Nr
Total Instrument Time: Unk/Nr

*** Note: NTSB investigators traveled in support of this investigation and used data obtained from various sources to prepare this aircraft accident report. ***

The airplane crashed about 4 miles southwest of the runway 5L threshold during an ILS approach. The captain had associated the illumination of the left engine IGN light, illuminated as a result of a momentary negative torque condition when the propeller speed levers were advanced tp 100% and the power levers were at flight idle, with an engine failure. There was no evidence of an engine failure. The captain failed to follow established procedures for engine failure identification, single engine approach, single engine go-around, and stall recovery. AMR Eagle training did not adequately address the recognition of engine failure at low power, the aerodynamic effects of asymmetric thrust from a 'windmilling' propeller and high thrust on the other engine. AMR Eagle and Flagship Airlines crew training records do not provide sufficient detail for management to track performance. Flagship Airlines management was deficient in its knowledge of the types of crew records available, and in the content and use of such records.

American Airlines Flight 965

Cali, Colombia

December 20, 1995

O N DECEMBER 20, 1995, AN American Airlines Boeing 757 air-craft with 163 crew and passengers crashed into the Andes Mountains, in hostile guerilla territory, just miles away from Cali, Colombia (CLO) at 8:42 p.m. (EST). Another accident. More people dead. I don't know what I felt when I received the call from AA CARE to activate me for the response. Only a year had passed since the crash of American Eagle 3379 in Raleigh-Durham, NC. I was numb.

Since the Raleigh-Durham accident, I had been promoted and now worked in Organizational Performance and Employee Development (OPED). I was one of six facilitators tasked with developing and facil-itating leadership training for managers and supervisors within the organization. OPED was also responsible for the CARE Program, AA's two-day family assistance training program. I was the only instructor who had ever been deployed so I was made the Program Manager of the CARE curriculum. Since joining OPED in early 1995 I had taught the CARE class numerous times. Now I was going to have to live it......again!

When I first joined American in 1982, I began my career with the airline as a reservation sales agent at the Southern Reservations Office (SRO) near the Dallas/Fort Worth International Airport (DFW). Considering my background in reservations and being familiar with the call center environment, I became a command center leader at the Telephone Enquiry Centre (TEC) during the Flight 965 activation. Another one of the facilitators from OPED would also be a TEC Leader with me during the response. There were several TEC Leaders so we could ensure twenty-four hour coverage. Little did we know when we began this deployment the command center would be open for almost two months.

All of us were dazed because the AMR family had experienced another accident. This was our first international accident response and we had no idea what differences we would encounter responding on foreign soil. Someone once said, "if you have seen one accident, you have seen one accident." There were similarities between the response for Flight 4184 and Flight 3379; however, this response would not look too much like the others. We learned of the 163 passengers and crew on board, there were at least four survivors as well as a dog in the cargo hold.

Many things were happening at AMR before this accident. AMR was growing and adding more planes, employees and destinations. The CARE Program had evolved into its own department and was in the midst of hiring a manager when the accident occurred. Unfortunately, this aspect of the response would add more anxiety than needed. The applicants for the CARE Program Manager's position were very anxious to prove their worth and each wanted to be in command of something. It became difficult for several of the leaders to actually lead as we were managing not only the response but the egos of the applicants as well. Unnecessary anxiety is never welcomed in an emergency.

As part of my initial command center duties, I was asked to coordinate the activation of CARE Team Members for deployment to Colombia. The notification and deployment process was still a paper process and very time consuming. Team members would call the volunteers to check on their availability. The challenge was finding people at home. Working for an airline, especially several days before Christmas, many employees where on vacation and away from home. Volunteers reached were weary of being activated having just responded to the two American Eagle accidents and still feeling the after shock. With this accident so close to a major holiday it was difficult to find volunteers to respond.

There were challenges in verifying the passenger manifest because of similar last names, families traveling together and passengers who may have provided a nickname rather than their legal name. In many cases, the passenger manifest did not match the name provided on the passport. In September 2001, after the 9/11 attacks, tighter controls were enacted regarding how names should be listed on reservations, tickets and boarding passes and this problem would be eliminated.

While verifying the passenger manifest, we quickly discovered there were entire families on the flight. In some cases only the head of the household remained at home, waiting to secure the house before departing to Cali for the holidays.

Another challenge we faced were family members needing to travel to Cali without proper credentials such as passports. Like the translation services, this task needed to be solved and a process established as quickly as possible. Thankfully, the American Airlines Government Affairs department representatives were able to work with the necessary stakeholders with the U.S. Department of State (DOS) to coordinate a means by which we could have a passport issued expeditiously or the family member would be allowed in to

Flight 965

PHOTO COURTESY OF: Curt Lewis, Curt Lewis and Associates, LLC

Colombia provided they possessed certain identification documents. It is important for an airline, or any organization, to establish these critical relationships and processes before having to respond to an event.

As part of the overall TEC responsibilities, we scheduled all passenger and CARE Team Member travel arrangements and accommodations. Once the arrangements were confirmed, copies of the itineraries would be sent to the board point, connecting point and off point of the flights. This insured the family members traveling would be met at each point of travel by an AA employee for escort to their flight. The escort would also advise the cockpit crew and the flight attendants that family members from the accident were on board the aircraft. This information also provided the downline station who was coming to their facility and where the families and team members would be housed.

Language would play a significant role in this response. CARE was still in its infancy. There were not enough Spanish-speaking team members to respond. We had to quickly determine how we would meet the need for Spanish speakers. Today, all the airlines are global carriers and there is no such thing as a local air carrier anymore. It is important now for an organization to tap into language translation services, assess their capabilities and be ready to respond to any passenger or crewmember regardless of their native language.

American mobilized command centers at AA Headquarters, the TEC, Dallas/Fort Worth International Airport (DFW), John F. Kennedy Airport (JFK), Miami International Airport (MIA), Alfonso Bonilla Aragon International Airport (CLO) as well as command centers at the hotels where team members and family members were staying, the morgue facility and several other locations. The various command centers stayed connected with each other by maintaining an open telephone bridge. We could all hear the various activities in each command center if their telephone line had not been muted. This provided an excellent way to ask questions, receive updates, and stay on top of the response.

At the base of the mountain where the plane crashed was a town called Buga. In a gymnasium type facility is where the morgue facility was stationed. The identification process was being performed by Colombian and United States officials. In addition to autopsies being performed, at one point, it was determined the bodies should be x-rayed for shrapnel to help determine if a terrorist act brought the plane down. This procedure delayed the identification and release of the bodies. Family members were getting angry because of the delay in the identification process. The families knew the bodies were in the building but no one had told them why there was a delay in the identification process. There was a fence surrounding the morgue

Flight 965

PHOTO COURTESY OF: Curt Lewis, Curt Lewis and Associates, LLC

facility for security purposes and people were pushing up against the fence trying to get into the facility. The situation was not safe and the facility needed to be evacuated. The TEC had an open bridge line to Buga. You could hear the urgency of our team members as they rushed to evacuate the building. It was a very tense situation. Good people, with good motives, just wanting to bury their family member(s). After this near riot took place, the x-rays stopped and the bodies identified were released. People came to the morgue in buses, trucks and even horse-drawn carriages to carry their loved one's body for burial. The morgue officials would post pictures of the deceased on a bulletin board and a family member(s) would see the photograph, verify it was their loved one and then take the body for burial. In some cases, family members were escorted into the morgue where all the bodies were if the picture was not enough for identification, to visually identify their loved one. There was no refrigeration system and the odor, sounds and sights were overwhelming for many of the families, CARE Team Members and other responders assigned to this post. Unless you work in the mortuary business I am not sure how prepared you can be to enter a room where over 160 bodies are being examined and stored. After the response to Flight 965, CARE Team Members would not be allowed into the morgue facility. If a family member asked their CARE Team Member to escort them to view the body, the CARE Team Member was instructed not to. Sharing the identification process of their presumed loved one was an extremely personal task which should only take place only with family members and morgue officials. The team member would stay behind and be available to support the family, once the returned from the viewing room facility.

In the TEC we received many telephone calls from family members with satellite phones who climbed the mountainside to find their family member at the accident scene. Once they arrived, they found looters rummaging through the wreckage for valuables, souvenirs and money. Souvenirs? What happened to human decency? According to one American Airlines's accident investigator, there was no security parameter set by the government or the army at the accident scene as to who could enter the accident site. Army soldiers were on scene to only maintain the peace and provide protection. The families with satellite phones would call our command center after locating their loved one in the wreckage and ask what they should do with the body. There was nothing in our manual on how to respond. What do you say to such a question? Several times the TEC received a call from a family member threatening to commit suicide. I had not heard of this happening in the prior two accident responses or of it even being reviewed in training. The grief of losing their entire family was overwhelming. The representatives taking the inbound calls would check with the caller to determine if they had a family member nearby or if there was someone we could call to be with them. If that was not a possibility we could call the police and stay on the line with the caller until the police arrived.

It had been one year and eight days since the crash of American Eagle 3379 in Raleigh-Durham, North Carolina. All of us were devastated to learn of the accident involving American Airlines flight 965. As bad as it sounds, the only question we kept asking, was why does this keep happening? In the year that had passed, processes and procedures were tightened and our response was becoming more efficient. However, this accident was not in the United States and the usual protections from our government were not present. The National Transportation Safety Board was not the lead investigation group, it was the Colombian government.

Flight 965

PHOTO COURTESY OF: Curt Lewis, Curt Lewis and Associates, LLC

There were many challenges in responding to flight 965. This was an accident on foreign soil, there were a large number of fatalities, and the accident occurred five days before Christmas. It was very challenging activating team members because many did not want to be away from home for Christmas. Additionally, as previously mentioned, our activation system was a simple, paper, call tree. One person from the activation team may call a volunteer but the information was not shared with the entire team. This simply added unnecessary work. Several days in to the response, I was at home after working a 12-hour shift when I received a call from the activation team asking if I was available to respond to the accident. I shook my head and said, "I have already been working four days, please stop calling to activate me, I am already active." This was my fifth activation call. Redesigning the activation and deployment process would later become one of the key processes to be addressed.

The plane crashed in active, hostile guerrilla territory. In order for American Airlines accident investigators and others to have safe passage to the accident site the Colombian military would escort the responders up the mountain. The team would get as close to the Colombian military base camp as they could. The Army location was approximately halfway up the mountain. From the basecamp, helicopters would be used to access the crash site.

We learned from the crash of Flight 965 to create an international data collector. The data collector contained questions concerning virtually every aspect of a response from accident investigation protocols, security requirements, to family assistance. Stations based outside the U.S. were asked to complete the data collector so if an event did occur off U.S. soil, the airline would be better prepared to handle the response by having information pertaining to the international accident location. Too bad we did not have the information before this accident.

On Christmas Eve, four days after the accident, the Colombian media stated alcohol had been found in the remains of the captain of Flight 965. We were all stunned to hear this news. Many CARE Team volunteers were saddened and felt extreme guilt for having to respond to an accident where the pilot may have been drinking and possibly causing the accident. As I've said before, unnecessary stress is not needed during a response. We would find out days later, the captain had not been drinking and the alcohol found in his system was due to the natural decomposition process. Too late however, the damage had been done. Family members heard the news about the alcohol found in the remains of the captain and were naturally angry and this anger was presented to the CARE Team Members working with them.

I'm not sure which is more challenging, working at your home base or at the accident site. One may think responding from your home base would be easier. You get to see your family, sleep in your own bed, and be surrounded by familiar things. For many of us this was simply not the case. Volunteers' children and, in some cases, even their spouses, expected them to be in the holiday spirit when we came home from work ready to shop, wrap presents, attend parties, and be in a festive mood. We were not. It became a challenge to go home. On Christmas Eve I brought holiday movies for volunteers to watch in the command center for the overnight shift. The TEC was open 24 hours a day and I worked the overnight shift. While we did not receive many calls overnight, the ones we did receive were usually from family members wanting to talk about how they were feeling and what they were experiencing.

For several of the CARE Team Members and Leaders, our deployment lasted almost two months. As mentioned earlier, in some cases, entire families and households were killed in the accident. The next-of-kin would need to travel to wherever the family was from to pack the house and close the estate. This took time to accomplish. In many cases, the CARE Team Member was released from working with the family, but the TEC would remain open as the central point of contact, hence the two month activation.

As the accident response finally began to wind down, we began to return to our everyday work, settling back into a routine was challenging. Many of us responded to three accidents within a 14-month period. In some cases, our families didn't understand why we would volunteer and our coworkers didn't understand either. This made transitioning from emergency response mode to being back home mode very challenging and, for some, depressing.

Several months after the response had ended there were rumors of having a recognition ceremony for the CARE Team volunteers who responded to Flight 965. This ceremony would never occur. Instead, the volunteers received a letter of commendation from a senior executive within the organization. I feel it is important to say; the volunteers within CARE perform this work because they care, not for company recognition. However, after responding to an accident so close to Christmas, being away from families and work, receiving a letter seemed like a slap in the face. We would later learn the discussion focused on whether or not CARE Team members should be reminded of the work just performed and in order to prevent any feelings from surfacing, senior management opted for the letter. Bad choice.

What was needed was the opportunity for the volunteers to unite, talk about their experiences, thank and hug each other, cry and grieve. This never happened. What a shame.

The crash of Flight 965 is not one I like to talk about. So many families were killed. Entire families flying home for the holidays gone in the blink of an eye. How devastating for those left behind. For the CARE Team volunteers, the response to Flight 965 was exhausting. I realized after this accident it isn't only survivors and family members who may experience traumatic stress, responders may as well. After this response, I was continually asked how I could respond again. Personally, I did not think I had a choice. I felt it was what I had to do. Needed to do. Many of the CARE Team Members felt the same as I did. However, we never, ever in our wildest dreams, thought we would be responding to three accidents in a 14 month period.

Lessons Learned

1 **If you have seen one accident, you have seen one accident.** While there were similarities in the response between Flights 4184, 3379 and 965 there were also many differences. No two accidents are the same.

2 **Priorities not procedures™.** Focus on the priorities. The procedures will fall in place. There needs to be flexibility within any procedure or process to adapt to any nuance to the response.

3 **Government Affairs.** Establish a relationship with your Government Affairs department within your organization. They will play an integral part in the response to an accident on foreign soil.

4 **Develop an International Data Collector.** Gather Information now about how the countries you serve will respond in the areas of accident investigations, humanitarian assistance, body identification and repatriation of remains. This information will be invaluable to you when you experience an event outside your home country.

5 **Translation services.** Today all airlines are global carriers. Tap in to language translation providers today to determine their capabilities to assist you when needed.

6 **Credentials.** Develop expedited credentialing protocols where possible. Not all the team members or family members you will

serve will have the proper documents necessary to travel to a foreign location. Establish guidelines with your Embassy and/or Consular for credentials in the event of an emergency.

7 **Security.** Establish security protocols for your response facilities. Consider having security guards or armed police at each center where families are briefed, the accident investigators gather to confer and the CARE Team Members are processed.

Flight 965

NTSB Identification: DCA96RA020

On December 20, 1995, American Airlines, Flight 965, a regularly scheduled passenger flight from Miami, Florida, to Cali, Colombia, crashed 38 miles north of Cali into mountainous terrain during a descent under instrument flight rules. There were 156 passengers and 8 crewmembers aboard. Four passengers survived the accident.

The accident was investigated by the Aeronautica Civil, Republica de Colombia. Assistance was provided by the NTSB under the provisions of Annex 13, Investigation of Accident and Incidents, to the Convention on International Civil Aviation.

In September 1996, the Aeronautica Civil issued a final report in which they determined that the Probable Causes of the Accident were:

1. The flightcrew's failure to adequately plan and execute the approach to runway 19 at SKCL and their inadequate use of automation.

2. Failure of the flightcrew to discontinue the approach into Cali, despite numerous cues alerting them of the inadvisability of continuing the approach.

3. The lack of situational awareness of the flightcrew regarding vertical navigation, proximity to terrain, and the relative location of critical radio aids.

4. Failure of the flightcrew to revert to basic radio navigation at the time when the FMS--- assisted navigation became confusing and demanded an excessive workload in a critical phase of the flight.

Any questions concerning the investigation must be referred to the Aeronautica Civil at Avenida El Dorado No. 106---95, Santafe' de Bogota', D.C., Colombia.

A copy of the final report issued by the Aeronautica Civil, Republica de Colombia report can be obtained by contacting:

NTSB Records Management Division
490 L'Enfant Plaza, SW
Washington, DC 20594
www.ntsb.gov

American Airlines Flight 1420

Little Rock, Arkansas
June 1, 1999

O N JUNE 1, 1999, AT 11:50 p.m. American Airlines Flight 1420 from Dallas-Fort Worth (DFW), Texas to Little Rock (LIT), Arkansas crashed when landing at the Little Rock international Airport. There were six crewmembers and 139 passengers on board. The flight had been delayed leaving Dallas-Fort Worth due to bad weather enroute. There were nine fatalities at the scene including the Captain of the flight. The First Officer, four flight attendants and 105 passengers had serious to minor injuries. 24 passengers were not injured. Two passengers would die several days after the accident due to their injuries.

Since the 1995 crash in Cali, Colombia, the CARE Program morphed into a formal department with a Manager and a Support Staff position. In early 1999, I was hired as a Senior Analyst for CARE and Emergency Response. I would continue to facilitate the CARE training class as well as create checklists for various procedures and streamline existing processes to ensure maximum efficiency and response effectiveness. Many enhancements had been made since the last accident in 1995. We now had an automated team member notification system, established team member assignment processes, and an organizational structure for the on-site response. However, the organizational structure was not complete and exercised when this accident occurred.

Flight 1420

The manager of the program called to inform me of the accident and requested I come to System Operations Control (SOC) as quickly as possible. The manager would take charge of the overall family assistance response and activities at SOC and I would deploy to Little Rock on the Go Team flight. The Go Team flight is comprised of various key departmental personnel needed to establish the command centers at the accident site. Department representatives from Corporate Communications, Risk Management, CARE, Safety, Maintenance and many others were on board. The Flight was scheduled to depart very early in the morning of June 2, several hours after receiving notification of the accident. There were two young girls on Flight 1420 who were from the DFW area. Their parents had called in to the Telephone Enquiry Centre and advised the representative their daughters were on board the accident aircraft. I am not sure who made the decision, but it was determined the parents of the girls would travel on board the Go Team flight to LIT. While it is very unusual to have family members on board this flight, it was the most expeditious way to get the parents to Little Rock. It was the right decision.

When the Go Team plane arrived in Little Rock we met with the General Manager of the AA LIT station and were briefed on what was happening at the current time, which was approximately 6:00 a.m. The accident investigators remained at the airport and I escorted the CARE Team volunteers to a hotel that would become our command center. We established a family assistance center at the airport and the CARE Team command center at the host hotel.

The command center was a large divided room which would hold the almost 300 team members on-site. While the room was large, it was a room divided by a large, dividing wall. On one side were the team leaders and the specialized functions like Risk Management, the Release Team, EAP and others. On the other side of the room, were round tables and an area for refreshments for the CARE Team. This was the working area and rest area for team members.

With almost 300 team members coming and going throughout the day, the entire room was quite noisy. Team members as well as leaders would continually say, "shhh" to quiet down the room. It would be quiet for a few minutes and the noise would build up again. Then you would hear, "shhhhhhhhh" again. Everyone was irritated every time they heard the "be quiet" sound. Our plan was to have a number of conference rooms for various activities; unfortunately we could not procure all the meeting space we needed. There were several conventions occurring in Little Rock when this accident happened and hotel meeting space was at a premium. We learned very quickly, procedures and plans do not always adhere to the circumstances at

Flight 1420

COURTESY OF THE: NTSB

hand. As I have mentioned previously, focus on the priorities. Look for other options to accomplish the task at hand. One of my favorite mantras is: Options Equal Success™.

I would brief the team members at least two times a day, once in the morning and once in the afternoon. In addition, other team leaders would also participate in the briefings to keep the volunteers informed of all activities. When a CARE Team Member had a question they were to see a team leader to discuss the question and the answer; however, the system initially proved not to work very well.

Why did the system not work? I had facilitated all of the CARE classes over the past several years and the volunteers were only comfortable talking with me because they knew me. After a briefing there would be a long line of volunteers waiting to see me. The NTSB would later recommend a more organized chain of command response structure. The complaint was it was difficult to reach me, or any of the Family Assistance Command Center Leaders, when needed. In addition, team members could potentially "shop" for answers. If they did not like what one team leader told them, they could go to another. After Flight 1420, we would strengthen our structure to follow the protocols of the Incident Command System (ICS).

The response to Flight 1420 was very different from the three previous accidents. Remember, every accident is different. Thankfully, Flight 1420 had more survivors than fatalities and this proved to be a challenging dynamic compared to previous responses. CARE Team volunteers were assigned to work with each survivor or family member(s) of a deceased passenger. Many of the volunteers would perform their work at local area hospitals, while those not injured would receive assistance at their home or by telephone. In addition, survivors and family members could receive information about the accident investigation and available services at the Family Assistance Center.

One of the service providers offered to the survivors and families were those of the American Red Cross (ARC). The ARC was very supportive during our response. The ARC coordinated access to spiritual care, child care, and emotional support among other services. These support services provide the opportunity for family members to have their children cared for and receive spiritual comfort without having to leave the Family Assistance Center where they may obtain information regarding the accident.

The crash of Flight 1420 was one of the first accidents by a major air carrier since the enactment of the Aviation Disaster Family Assistance Act of 1996 (The Act). Most of us viewed our response as a test of how we met the Assurances as listed in the Act. While AA had a well-established Family Assistance Plan, the Act actually removed several tasks previously performed by the air carrier. For example, death notification and conducting an ante mortem interview were no longer performed by the airline. These duties would fall to the local Coroner or Medical Examiner. Where the local authorities could not perform these functions due to manpower issues, the Disaster Mortuary Operations Response Team (DMORT) may be brought in to assist the local authorities. The NTSB was now responsible for not only the accident investigation but also for ensuring the airline and other key stakeholders fulfilled the requirements of the Act.

This was the first time for American to work with the NTSB Transportation Disaster Assistance personnel. Many of those involved in the family assistance response of Flight 1420 were following the new guidelines set forth in the Act. Coordination of activities was challenging at first. We were all learning our way. For example, at the first briefing at the Family Assistance Center, the airline representative, which was going to address the passengers and families, was replaced at the last minute. The airline Chief Accident Investigator would now brief the families from an airline standpoint. There was no discussion on what would be covered or how long the briefing would last. No one really knew what to expect.

Another reason Flight 1420 was different was because of the number of survivors. Until this accident, most air carriers planned for what was referred to as the "worst case scenario" which was an all fatality accident. However, the industry as a whole had not planned on how to respond to an accident where there were so many survivors. Many of the tasks performed and services requested in the aftermath of an air disaster were the same regardless if there are survivors or fatalities. However, there are differences.

A huge difference from the previous accident responses was the dispersing of the survivors. While passengers and crew were sent to

Flight 1420

COURTESY OF THE: NTSB

local area hospitals, many people were not physically injured and left the airport for home. One survivor found his way to a hotel near the airport and it was not until the next day the airline was able to locate him. Hospitals were reluctant to provide information due to privacy reasons, and this was before HIPPA was enacted. Everyone involved did what they could to determine the location of all the passengers and crew as quickly as possible but it did take time.

Another difference were multiple requests from survivors who wanted to come to LIT Airport and sit in the same seat they sat in on the accident flight. While this is not an unreasonable request, aircraft often fly in and fly out of a location with little down time, hampering the passengers' request. In addition, not all aircraft flown by American into LIT were MD-82's, like the accident aircraft, contributing to the challenges of helping the survivors fulfill their request. I admired how passengers were doing what they could to conquer their fears and emotions after the accident. I was amazed yet again at the resiliency of the survivors and the responders. One way to understand the differences is to have survivors and family members of accidents attend your corporate emergency response training. Learn first hand from the survivors and the families who have experienced what you are preparing for.

Another difference focused on the family members of survivors. After returning home, for example, I received a number of requests from survivors for counseling for their family members. One survivor told me his family thought he should "be over it," meaning, since he survived, he should be thankful and move on with his life. He was not over it. He would go to bed and the images of the aircraft speeding down the runway and the fire that engulfed the aircraft after it came to a stop was haunting him. His family did not have to experience those sights. But the survivor did.

Another difference centered on the return of luggage and personal belongings. Passengers wanted their carryon bags and their luggage back. Unfortunately, many of those items had been burned in the fire and may have also been contaminated by jet fuel, fire retardant or blood borne pathogens. Belongings could not just be returned. They needed to be "safe to handle" before they could be returned. American brought in a Fort Worth, Texas-based company to collect, inventory, clean and return the items to passengers. This process would take some time.

It is very important for an organization to understand the role and capabilities of their vendors. Thankfully, American had established a relationship with the personal effects vendor after experiencing three previous accidents. Until the carry-on and checked luggage was returned, the airline provided a monetary payment of $25,000 for each person on board the aircraft. The purpose of the money was for survivors, and the families of those who lost a loved one on the flight, to take care of everyday expenses without having to ask their CARE Team Member for money. The advance payment would provide some initial financial flexibility for those impacted by the crash. The team members provided each survivor and family member a letter explaining the advance payment was not a settlement or that it precluded them from taking legal action. However, some survivors would not cash the check and others, while they would cash the check, still requested American to pay their out of pocket expenses, which the airline did.

This was the first time American Airlines had provided an advance payment. Questions regarding the payment focused on if the money was taxable from the Internal Revenue Service (IRS) and as I mentioned earlier, did cashing the check mean accepting it as a settlement? Have your corporate legal department draft a template today for any advance payment you may provide. Make sure the letter is direct, answers questions you anticipate a survivor or family member may have had and, most of all, that it is written with compassion and empathy for the situation.

The site visit for the survivors and family members provided an additional challenge. The site was off a runway, down an embankment, close to the river. The logistics of scheduling the site visit were numerous. The NTSB, the American Red Cross and American Airlines worked closely together to address logistical issues such as: how close should everyone be permitted to be to the site? What time of day for the site visit would air operations would be least impacted? What kind of security needed to be provided since people would be on the airfield? All of these challenges were addressed and the site visit did occur. The personal belongings vendor ceased their operation and removed their crews out of respect for those attending the site visit. Many of the survivors and family of those who died left a keepsake on bales of hay, which served as a parameter barrier, to memorialize their loved one or the fact they survived.

During one of the briefings, I asked the CARE Team volunteers how many were first time responders. Almost 80 per cent were new. Our goal was to partner an experienced CARE Team Member with a new team member. However, CARE is a voluntary organization and it was the new team members who volunteered. This is another reason why you need to keep your processes flexible!

I remember there were a number of CARE Team Member challenges during the response to AA Flight 1420. One was a team member who told me she needed to be released from duty. I asked her why. Her response surprised me. She said she was retiring from the company and the next day was her last day. Seriously! I could not believe what I was hearing. I thanked her for her service, released her and found a new team member to work with her partner while they continued to assist the family. What a disservice to the family who may have already built a bond of sorts with the team only for it to be disrupted because someone was retiring. I was very incensed this team member even activated for deployment knowing she was going to retire.

One team member came to me in tears and asked if she could speak to me. We found a conference room and I asked her what was wrong thinking she might be experiencing difficulties with her CTM partner or the family she was assigned. This was not the case. She told me she had just been on the phone with her husband. He was upset because she was not back home yet and he had to take care of their young daughter. He told his wife she had abandoned them. She was very upset over the conversation. I would be too. It was what she said next that really surprised me. She said, "I do not know if I can be married to someone who does not get what we do." I did not know what to say to her. I gave her a hug and we just sat there together for a few minutes. I do not know if she stayed married to her husband or not.

The family assistance response on scene in LIT was a little more than 14 days. The immediate needs of the passengers on board and the crew had been taken care of, long-term care for those who were still in the hospital or in rehabilitation had been addressed and it was now time to leave.

There were so many team members released on the same day, I worked with AA SOC to fly in a Boeing 757 to LIT in order to get everyone home. Otherwise, as the commercial flights were nearly full, team members would have had to wait for days for a flight home.

American allowed each team member to have one day off for each day of activation time up to five days. This extra time off was to help the team member decompress and get back into their home life before returning to work. Some team members went back to work immediately, although we suggested against it. However, I would come to learn going back to work right away was just what a team member may need. A return to normalcy! It depends on the individual.

After I got home, my manager, our support staff representative and I spent many days and months reviewing what worked well and what did not during the Flight 1420 response. In addition, we held several debriefs with team members and leaders to glean what they liked and did not like about the operation. We continued to fine-tune our processes and procedures based on what we learned and heard from all of the stakeholders involved. The challenge? Each accident brings a new set of considerations not previously thought of. To say the least, the work for any emergency response department never ends.

Lessons Learned

1   **Processes and procedures are never finished.** They are living documents which must be flexible enough to adapt to the various logistics which may have been previously not been planned for.

2   **Emergency response plans must be flexible.** Depending on the location and the time of an emergency, logistical challenges such as a closed airport, not enough hotel rooms, no electricity, poor Internet connection and so forth could significantly impact your response.

3   **CTM availability.** Not all your team member volunteers are going to be available when you need them. While it is preferred to have processes where a male and female will be paired together or an experienced team member with an inexperienced team member, that may not always happen.

4   **Vendors (3rd party service providers).** Include your vendors for personal belongings recovery, repatriation of remains, environmental cleanup and any other vendor you may have in your exercises.

5   **Passenger and crew tracking.** It is imperative an organization has a good understand of how local authorities will triage and track the people impacted by the disaster. Each location may be different in how they handle mass casualty situations. Better to explore this issue before a disaster occurs.

6   **Survivors.** The needs of survivors are sometimes different than the needs of a family who lost a loved one in the accident. Invite survivors to your training program. Ask them for their input as to what plans need to be made for survivors.

7   **Advance payment.** Prepare your advance payment letter now. Determine the amount of money for the advancement payment as well. Write the letter and vet it through your insurance, legal and tax department for content and accuracy.

Flight 1420

Executive Summary

On June 1, 1999, at 2350:44 central daylight time, American Airlines flight 1420, a McDonnell Douglas DC-9-82 (MD-82), N215AA, crashed after it overran the end of runway 4R during landing at Little Rock National Airport in Little Rock, Arkansas. Flight 1420 departed from Dallas/Fort Worth International Airport, Texas, about 2240 with 2 flight crewmembers, 4 flight attendants, and 139 passengers aboard and touched down in Little Rock at 2350:20. After departing the end of the runway, the airplane struck several tubes extending outward from the left edge of the instrument landing system localizer array, located 411 feet beyond the end of the runway; passed through a chain link security fence and over a rock embankment to a flood plain, located approximately 15 feet below the runway elevation; and collided with the structure supporting the runway 22L approach lighting system. The captain and 10 passengers were killed; the first officer, the flight attendants, and 105 passengers received serious or minor injuries; and 24 passengers were not injured. The airplane was destroyed by impact forces and a postcrash fire. Flight 1420 was operating under the provisions of 14 Code of Federal Regulations Part 121 on an instrument flight rules flight plan.

The National Transportation Safety Board determines that the probable causes of this accident were the flight crew's failure to discontinue the approach when severe thunderstorms and their associated hazards to flight operations had moved into the airport area and the crew's failure to ensure that the spoilers had extended after touchdown. Contributing to the accident were the flight crew's (1) impaired performance resulting from fatigue and the situational stress associated with the intent to land under the circumstances, (2) continuation of the approach to a landing when the company's maximum crosswind component was exceeded, and (3) use of reverse thrust greater than 1.3 engine pressure ratio after landing.

The safety issues in this report focus on flight crew performance, flight crew decision-making regarding operations in adverse weather, pilot fatigue, weather information dissemination, emergency response, frangibility of airport structures, and Federal Aviation Administration (FAA) oversight. Safety recommendations concerning these issues are addressed to the FAA and the National Weather Service.

Flight 1420

National Transportation Safety Board
Washington, DC 20594

Brief of Accident

Adopted 05/28/2002

Printed on : 11/23/2014 02:32:29 PM

DCA99MA060
File No. 11847

06/01/1999   LITTLE ROCK, AR   Aircraft Reg No. N215AA   Time (Local): 23:51 CDT

Make/Model: Mcdonnell Douglas/MD-82
Engine Make/Model: P&W / JT8D-217C
Aircraft Damage: Destroyed
Number of Engines: 2
Operating Certificate(s): Flag Carrier/Domestic
Name of Carrier: AMERICAN AIRLINES INC
Type of Flight Operation: Scheduled; Domestic; Passenger Only
Reg Flight Conducted Under: Part 121: Air Carrier

	Fatal	Serious	Minor/None
Crew	1	4	1
Pass	10	41	88

Last Depart. Point: DFW, TX
Destination: Same as Accident/Incident Location
Airport Proximity: On Airport/Airstrip
Airport Name: ADAMS FIELD
Runway Identification: 4R
Runway Length/Width (Ft): 7200 / 150
Runway Surface: Concrete
Runway Surface Condition: Wet

Condition of Light: Night
Weather Info Src: Weather Observation Facility
Basic Weather: Instrument Conditions
Lowest Ceiling: 5000 Ft AGL, Overcast
Visibility: 1.00 SM
Wind Dir/Speed: 280 / 018 kts
Temperature (°C): 19
Precip/Obscuration:

Pilot-in-Command   Age: 48

Certificate(s)/Rating(s)
Airline Transport; Multi-engine Land

Instrument Ratings

Flight Time (Hours)

Total All Aircraft: 10234
Last 90 Days: 54
Total Make/Model: Unk/Nr
Total Instrument Time: Unk/Nr

*** Note: NTSB investigators traveled in support of this investigation and used data obtained from various sources to prepare this aircraft accident report. ***

The full report (NTSB/AAR-01-02) is available on the NTSB Web site. See http://www.ntsb.gov/publictn/publictn.htm for details.

On June 1, 1999, at 2350:44 central daylight time, American Airlines flight 1420, a McDonnell Douglas DC-9-82 (MD-82), N215AA, crashed after it overran the end of runway 4R during landing at Little Rock National Airport in Little Rock, Arkansas. Flight 1420 departed from Dallas/Fort Worth International Airport, Texas, about 2240 with 2 flight crewmembers, 4 flight attendants, and 139 passengers aboard and touched down in Little Rock at 2350:20. After departing the end of the runway, the airplane struck several tubes extending outward from the left edge of the instrument landing system (ILS) localizer array, located 411 feet beyond the end of the runway; passed through a chain link security fence and over a rock embankment to a flood plain, located approximately 15 feet below the runway elevation; and collided with the structure supporting the runway 22L approach lighting system. The captain and 10 passengers were killed; the first officer, the flight attendants and 105 passengers received serious or minor injuries; and 24 passengers were not injured.2 The airplane was destroyed by impact forces and a postcrash fire. Flight 1420 was operating under the provisions of 14 Code of Federal Regulations (CFR) Part 121 on an instrument flight rules (IFR) flight plan.

American Airlines Flight 11

New York City, New York

American Airlines Flight 77

Washington, D.C.

September 11, 2001

I N EARLY 2001, I HAD been promoted from Senior Analyst to Manager of CARE and Emergency Response. One of my first priorities as Manager was to create a corporate emergency response working group. After experiencing five accidents since 1993, it was past time to build a working group of all the internal stakeholders who would respond to an accident. The former manager of the program had the idea to build a group but had recently left American to pursue other endeavors. I thought he had a good idea and would move forward with it. In addition, it was a priority to hire someone to fill my previous position as Senior Analyst. It took several months to interview and select a replacement. Once we had completed the lengthy hiring process and the new analyst was on board, the next several months were spent training and teaching her how to instruct the CARE class along with numerous other job responsibilities.

Most everyone remembers what he or she was doing on September 11, 2001. The new Senior Analyst and I were beginning to facilitate the two day CARE class with approximately 25 participants. We were teaching in the Officer Conference Room at the American Airlines Headquarters building.

I can only imagine the new Senior Analyst was nervous to teach the class for the first time, especially with her new boss there. The class began at 8:00 a.m. and she would teach the *Introduction to CARE* section, which would take until approximately 9:30 a.m. I have to say; she was doing an exceptional job for her first class when, at approximately 8:40 a.m., the telephone rang in the conference room. I motioned for her to continue and I went to answer the phone. Our support staff representative told me to cancel the class because one of our planes had hit the World Trade Center in New York City. I must not have said anything because she said, "Ken, did you hear what I said?" My mind was processing the various possibilities. She went on to say the plane had been hijacked and had been flown into the building. The entire air system was being shut down by order of the Federal Aviation Administration (FAA). Her complete instructions were to cancel the class and get to SOC immediately. I hung up the phone, interrupted my colleague and advised the class we needed to step out of the room for a few minutes. I told my colleague what happened, we walked back into the room and explained the situation to the class. We left and went directly to SOC.

The horrible events of 9/11 are permanently embedded in most people's minds. Working for American Airlines only compounded the fear, chaos and emotions we were all experiencing within the American family. Upon arrival at SOC, our team went to work opening the CARE Operations Center, while I was briefed with updated information from the SOC Managing Director. We arrived just minutes before the first of the two World Trade Center buildings collapsed. Flight 11 with 11 crewmembers, 76 passengers and five hijackers on board and from Boston, Massachusetts to LAX was the first plane to hit the World Trade Center followed by United Airlines Flight 175, which hit the second tower.

Media reports of a plane hitting the Pentagon in Washington, D.C. were now starting to be shown on television but there was no confirmation about which airline was involved. We would later learn it was AA Flight 77 with six crewmembers and 58 passengers, including five hijackers, from Washington, D.C., Dulles International Airport (IAD) to Los Angeles International Airport (LAX) in California. The American Airlines Chief Accident Investigator happened to be in Washington, D.C. on September 11, 2001. He was in D.C. to attend an FAA and NTSB meeting regarding Flight Data Recorders (FDR) and Cockpit Voice Recorders (CVR), and after being briefed about Flight 11 being flown into the World Trade Center, he immediately headed to Ronald Reagan Washington National Airport (DCA) for a flight to New York City. He shared with me the following; "I was in a cab going from downtown to National (DCA) when I saw it explode. I sensed something, looked off to my right, I saw a fireball come up out of the Pentagon, felt the shockwave in the cab and then I heard it." Ultimately, he remained in D.C. to respond to the terrorist event and he visually identified wreckage from the aircraft, confirming it was Flight 77.

While the Aviation Disaster Family Act of 1996 (The Act) was not invoked because 9/11 was a terrorist event, AA would follow the priorities of The Act for its overall response.

9/11, World Trade Center, New York City, NY

AP Images

I briefed my team and we began the notification and activation process for CARE Team volunteers. We used an automated notification system which utilized 16 modem lines to generate phone calls to the team members we designated. We recorded our message and sent an all-hands notification call-out to the volunteers. When a team member received a call they would follow the prompts provided by the notification system and advise if they were available for deployment. Team members also had the ability to call the CARE command center directly utilizing a phone number provided on their CARE Team identification badge. The problem? The headquarter campus phone system failed. American Airlines (at the time) had approximately 30,000 employees plus their families living and working in the Dallas/Fort Worth area. Everyone from employees to family members of employees were calling each other. Adding calls from the other 50,000 company wide employees not in the area simply overloaded the system and it failed. In short, we could reach out to our team members because the modem lines we used were not affiliated with the phone system. However, none of our team members could call us.

The American Airlines CARE Team Members are comprised of volunteers throughout the organization. In previous activations we were able to achieve the staffing levels we needed for an effective response but it would prove to be a challenge with this response. The fear of another terrorist event was overwhelming. Team members did not want to leave their families. Employees were scared. Their families were scared for them. Many did not want to fly. I understood their fears. I was experiencing the same fear. What is your plan for lack of manpower? How will you respond if you are not able to achieve your designated manpower levels?

In a normal (is there such a thing?) deployment situation, the airlines Go Team flight would be wheels up within three hours of notification of an event. 9/11 was anything but normal! I do not know how our SOC was able to get approval but they managed to arrange four flights to the impacted locations, which included the origin of the flights, which were Boston, Massachusetts and Washington, D.C., and the destination of the flights which was Los Angeles, California, and New York City, New York where Flight 11 had been flown into the World Trade Center. American would establish Family Assistance

Centers in each of these cities. Considering the difficulty with the phone system, which took several hours to correct, the system failure turned out to be a blessing in disguise. We had additional time to work through our procedures, activate team members, and fly to the four destinations mentioned. Normally SOC, the Safety Department and CARE would determine who would be on the initial Go-Flight and additional team members would follow on later flights. As I previously mentioned, this was not a normal activation and we would have to modify our existing procedures for deployment. Once it was determined who would be on each of the flights, full names, addresses, birth dates, Social Security numbers and passport numbers would have to be provided to the government and passengers cleared before any of the flights could depart. If memory serves me, all four flights departed around 4:00 p.m. in the afternoon. Onboard each of the planes with the American employees were representatives from the Federal Aviation Administration (FAA), the Federal Bureau of Investigation (FBI) and other government representatives. CARE leadership was divided between three locations. I went to New York City and my new Senior Analyst went to Los Angeles. My other Senior Analyst and Support Staff Representative stayed at the CARE Command Center to run the HDQ operation.

It was an unusual Go Team flight because of the attacks of 9/11 and the overwhelming enormity of the event. Not only had terrorists struck the United States but also American Airlines planes and United Airlines planes had been used as weapons of mass destruction. We had heard flight attendants from the affected aircraft had called dispatch to explain the horror of what was going on inside the plane. This only added to the emotions we were already experiencing. As we made our approach to New York City, the Captain of our aircraft announced U.S. fighter jets were escorting us. A CARE Team volunteer

9/11, The Pentagon, Washington, D.C.

AP Images

sitting a few seats away from me said something to the effect of "I am glad we have a safe escort to the city." Someone sitting next to her said, "They are not escorting us, they are there to shoot us down if we go off course." I remember thinking, "What am I doing on this plane?" When we landed at New York City's LaGuardia International Airport (LGA), the aircraft immediately taxied to the gate. It was the first time I ever arrived at LGA so quickly. We were transferred to the host hotel where our command center and team members would be housed. Thankfully, with several team members in the New York City area, they were able to go to the hotel in advance of our arrival and to begin to set up the command center.

In Washington, D.C. we were fortunate to have several CARE Team Members in the Washington, D.C. area. They were willing to be deployed and were instrumental in establishing and running the

CARE Command Center in D.C. Later the Department of Defense (DoD) would establish a large family assistance center in Crystal City, Virginia. Crew members and passenger family members were welcomed at the DoD FAC. While this created a challenge in coordinating activities between the 2 locations, it was not impossible. The DoD provided excellent services for those employees and military affected by the events of 9/11 and were gracious enough to include the families of Flight 77.

Security was a priority! All of our command centers system-wide had armed guards at the entry points. All CARE Team Members and other responders were required to provide appropriate credentials each time they entered. If a center had windows, they were to be covered. In a "normal" accident response situation, family members would travel to the accident site location and receive information from key stakeholders at the designated family assistance center. That did not happen in this response. Family members could not travel to the various locations as the air system was completely shut down. Unless they lived or drove to where a family assistance center was set up, the majority of the family assistance work was performed by telephone. If family members did arrive at a family assistance center our team members could only provide assistance in a secured location such as the family assistance center itself or where an armed guard had secured additional locations. Providing CARE assistance at their homes was not permitted for security purposes.

Navigating the CARE Team family assistance response was very challenging. FBI representatives were stationed at the American Airlines SOC and the FBI representatives would advise us which families we could and could not talk to. Until the FBI had vetted all passengers and crew of the flights, each was considered a suspect. When there is a tragedy such as an aircraft disaster, family, friends and coworkers call the airline that had the accident. The Telephone Enquiry Center for AA had been provided the passenger and crew list for flight 11 and 77. After several hours of receiving phone calls it was obvious to us who the potential hijackers were for each of the American Airlines flights because no one had called for them. With the hijackers potentially known, everyone else on the plane still needed to be cleared by the FBI.

I am sure the FBI and other governmental representatives worked as expeditiously as possible to clear the remaining passengers and crew. However mistakes were made. There were times when the FBI would say a passenger was cleared and we could talk with their family only to have the FBI place the passenger back on the "do not call list" hours or days later. One passenger's family, in particular, had this happen several times. The last time it happened, AA respectfully asked the FBI to contact the family because they were putting the airline in a precarious position. In addition, FBI headquarters had requested any FBI field office requests for the passenger and crew manifest be directed to HDQ for approval and distribution. However, it did not stop FBI field offices from calling me or other command center leaders asking for the list and threatening arrest if we did not provide it to them. I explained I was following FBI established protocols, provided a phone number for the field representative to call to request the manifest and eventually the requests stopped.

Considering the enormity of 9/11, the families we worked with in person and on the telephone appreciated the information and assistance the CARE Team members provided. Some families would drive to an FAC, others would take a train if seats were available, but most remained at home. They knew what happened, this was no accident, and the United States had been attacked. As with previous accidents, American Airlines provided an initial payment of $25,000 to the families of those killed on the planes. This money was to help with funeral and household costs along with other necessary expenditures they may have. If the family needed additional monies they could request those from their CARE Team Members. Typically we would present the check in person with a letter of explanation but in this case it was not possible. We would utilize FedEx ground services to deliver the checks until the airline system was back online.

All of our locations where Family Assistance Center's were established were operating well. After several days, the air system began to come online. Only a small percentage of flights at first, followed by a few more flights each day. I was asked to fly home and coordinate the closing of the centers from my office at SOC. When I arrived at LaGuardia Airport there were no passengers in the ticketing part of the terminal except for the ticket agents. I had never seen this airport empty, it was very surreal. I checked in for my flight, went through security with no line and walked to my departure gate. I was flying home on a Boeing 757 aircraft. The plane held 188 passengers between First Class and the Main Cabin. There were only nine passengers on board including me; four in First Class and five in the Main Cabin. I was upgraded to First Class before boarding. When I boarded the flight, the First Class flight attendant sat next to me before takeoff and said "If there's a problem with any passenger on this plane I am coming to you for help." I guess I wouldn't be having a double vodka on this flight after all! I remember sitting in the waiting area looking at the other eight passengers and wondering why I had not taken the train home. I answered my own question by thinking it would look bad for the manager of emergency response for a major airline to take the train home versus the plane. I have never been afraid to fly before and was determined I would not let what happened on 9/11 scare me from flying.

During the 9/11 response, it was important for American and United Airlines to coordinate activities together. There is no competition in emergency response. Our command centers maintained similar operating hours, travel guidelines for families were the same, and we coordinated the timing of advance payments to families as well. Several weeks after the tragic events of 9/11 American and United worked together with the city of New York government officials and the American Red Cross to have a site visit for the families of the flights flown into the World Trade Center.

A short time after I returned home and all the Family Assistance Centers had closed; questions from family members were routed through the airline Telephone Enquiry Center. It was a good way for family members to keep in touch with the airline. One aspect of the 9/11 tragedy, which surprised us because it had not happened in our previous responses, was the outpouring of support from charitable and private organizations, as well as donations from school children. In addition, American and United were inundated with requests for family addresses from organizations to send various items to recognize the loss the families experienced. The items included things such as greeting cards, American flags, hand drawn pictures, flag boxes, memory books, and donations of money. The families were very appreciative of all the items; however, at one point it became overwhelming. Neither airline would provide personal information to the organization requesting it. We would ask the organization making the donation to send their item to us and we would forward it to each family. After receiving donated items, several families requested we send items to them once a week or once a month because receiving them almost every day was too emotional. We were happy to honor their request. The outpouring of gifts, cards, letters, money and other items was to honor those who had died and reflected the goodness of the human spirit.

During this tumultuous time, the airline industry was rapidly losing money. As a result of this, there was a significant possibility of layoffs of airline employees across the entire industry, including employees from American and United Airlines. In the United States, before a company with over 100 or more employees conducts a massive layoff, the Worker Adjustment and Retraining Notification Act (WARN Act) mandates the company must first send out a WARN letter to employees advising of a potential layoff. The letter must be sent out sixty calendar days in advance of mass layoffs. Because the airlines were losing so much money and mass layoffs were a possibility, WARN letters needed to be sent immediately.

One can only imagine the emotion of a CARE Team member receiving such a letter while helping families in the aftermath of such horrific proportions. Employees were now faced with making a decision. If they remained working with a family, would their manager consider them expendable because they were not in the office, or, did the employee need to stop their family assistance work and go home to reestablish their value to the work group? To say the least, this was an aspect of emergency response we had never had to contend with in the past. Due to the tragedy of 9/11 and the immediate decline of air travel, thousands of employees were laid off, including many from American and United, who were helping families of 9/11.

As with any aircraft accident or disaster the positive identification of each passenger and crewmember is an important part of the response and, for the families impacted, part of healing. When it came to identifying the people on board the four planes used as weapons of mass destruction, each had its own challenges. In some cases positive identification was made for each passenger and crewmember and for others the identification process continued for over 10 years. I cannot imagine the emotion and feelings family members must have experienced when receiving a call from the Medical Examiner that their loved one had been identified after all those years.

The terrorist attacks of September 11, 2001 were tragic. So many people killed. Planes used as weapons of mass destruction. No one ever thought this would happen to the United States. However, what I learned from the attacks was similar to what I had experienced in previous accidents. The resilient spirit of the families and those who responded on that fateful day is nothing short of heroic. I was in awe of the compassion of the families we all worked with, and the airline team members who put their fear aside and traveled during a very challenging time to help families who lost loved ones. Also amazing were the citizens of the U.S. and many other countries, which sent donations of money, gifts and cards to the families of those who died and about the collaborative response from all the government agencies involved.

Lessons Learned

1 **A terrorist event completely changes the accident response playing field.** Establish your key stakeholder relationships with all government agencies not just the NTSB.

2 **Emotions were different.** While grieving the loss of those who died on each of the aircraft, there was the additional grief of this being a terrorist event and thousands of people being killed in the World Trade Center. September 11, 2001 was a sentinel event that impacted people on a global basis.

3 **The air system was shut down.** Our response plans had to be adapted to what we could and could not do with regards to communicating with passenger and crew families.

4 **Security.** Determine if you will use off-duty police or a security firm for your response centers. Coordinate this activity with your corporate security department.

5 **Donations.** Determine in advance how your organization will address donations if you receive them.

6 **Manpower.** How will you adapt your family assistance response if you do not achieve your staffing goals? Our response changed from an in-person to primarily a telephone response.

7   **Employee issues.** In a terrorist event or an accident where your employees have been injured or killed, who within your organization is best to respond to the situation? Examine very closely the impact of an employee responding to the death of employees they work with. They may be too close to the situation to handle it emotionally. In some cases, having a company representative from another department respond may be more appropriate. You may also consider bringing in a third party vendor, not affiliated with your organization, to respond.

8   **Debriefs.** Mandatory or voluntary? After the events of 9/11 a number of studies were released recommending voluntary debriefs, defusings and Critical Incident Stress Debriefs (CISD) rather than mandatory. Determine this process now.

Flight 11

NATIONAL TRANSPORTATION SAFETY BOARD
Vehicle Recorders Division
Washington, D.C. 20594

December 21, 2001

Air Traffic Control Recording

Specialist's Report
by Joseph A. Gregor

A. ACCIDENT

Location:	New York, New York
Date:	September 11, 2001
Time:[1]	
Aircraft:	Boeing 767-200ER
NTSB Number:	DCA01SA060

B. GROUP

N/A

C. SUMMARY

On September 11, 2001 American Airlines Flight 11, a Boeing 767 crashed into Tower 1 of the World Trade Center in New York City, New York. A certified analog copy of air traffic control (ATC) transmissions recorded on September 11, 2001 at various tower, departure, and Air Route Traffic Control Center (ARTCC) positions along the route of flight was sent to the audio laboratory of the National Transportation Safety Board. These recordings were used to create an audio track and text transcript of the aircraft-ground communications from takeoff to accident time.

Flight 11

- ii -

D. DETAILS OF INVESTIGATION

Transmissions between the accident aircraft and ATC were recorded and an analog copy was sent to the Safety Board's audio laboratory. The tapes cover the following ATC positions and time periods:

Facility	Time Period[1] (UTC)	Position
BOS	1152:37 – 1217:48	LCE
BOS	1155:32 – 1210:49	ID (B)
	1157:42 – 1210:00	SL
ZBW	1205:32 – 1208:50	Sector 47R
ZBW	1204:51 – 1233:59	Sector 46R

Sections of the tape recordings containing air-ground transmissions to and from the incident aircraft were digitized at a 22,050 Samples/second data rate and saved as standard Microsoft .wav files. Individual .wav files were combined into a single 35 minute 12 second long .wav file containing all transmissions to and from the incident aircraft from 1159:02 UTC (aircraft cleared for takeoff) to 1234:14. A transcript was obtained from the final composite recording. Times are approximate due to limitations inherent in the data obtained from the FAA.

Joseph A. Gregor
Electrical Engineer

Flight 11

- iii -

Transcript of ATC communications with a Boeing B-767-200ER (American Airlines flight 11) which crashed into Tower 1 of the World Trade Center in New York City, New York on September 11, 2001.

LEGEND

AAL-11	Radio transmission from American B-767-200ER, flight 11
LCE	Radio transmission from Local Control East
ID (B)	Radio transmission from Initial Departure position B
SL	Radio transmission from Lincoln Departure
47R	Radio transmission from Sector 47 Radar position
46R	Radio transmission from Sector 46 Radar position
*	Unintelligible word
#	Expletive
( )	Questionable insertion
[ ]	Editorial insertion
...	Pause
—	Interruption

Note 1: Times are expressed in universal coordinated time (UTC).

Note 2: Only radio transmissions to and from the accident aircraft were transcribed.

Note 3: Words shown with excess vowels, letters, or drawn out syllables are a phonetic representation of the words as spoken.

Flight 11

Time	Station	Transmission
1159:02	LCE	American eleven heavy traffic's orbiting north of the field at thirty five hundred feet maintain three thousand runway four right, cleared for takeoff. [BOS 11:52-1217 LCE]
1159:11	AAL-11	maintain three cleared for takeoff on four right. what are the winds? [BOS 11:52-1217 LCE]
1159:14	LCE	wind three three zero at niner. [BOS 11:52-1217 LCE]
1159:16	AAL-11	***. [BOS 11:52-1217 LCE]
1200:11	LCE	American eleven heavy contact departure that traffic's now in your ten o'clock and two miles thirty four hundred feet. [BOS 11:52-1217 LCE]
1200:19	AAL-11	* we have him in sight and going to departure so long American eleven heavy. [BOS 11:52-1217 LCE]
1200:30	AAL-11	departure good morning American eleven heavy with you passing through ah two thousand for three thousand. [BOS 11:55-1210 Initial Dept.]
1200:36	ID (B)	American eleven heavy Boston departure radar contact good morning traffic ten o'clock two miles maneuvering Cessna Skylane VFR at three thousand five hundred. [BOS 11:55-1210 Initial Dept.]
1200:43	AAL-11	we have him in sight American eleven. [BOS 11:55-1210 Initial Dept.]
1201:19	ID (B)	American eleven heavy climb and maintain eight thousand. [BOS 11:55-1210 Initial Dept.]
1201:21	AAL-11	eight thousand American eleven heavy. [BOS 11:55-1210 Initial Dept.]
1202:14	ID (B)	American eleven heavy turn right heading one eight zero. [BOS 11:55-1210 Initial Dept.]
1202:16	AAL-11	one eighty American eleven heavy. [BOS 11:55-1210 Initial Dept.]
1203:03	ID (B)	American eleven heavy climb and maintain one four thousand. [BOS 11:55-1210 Initial Dept.]
1203:06	AAL-11	one four thousand American eleven heavy. [BOS 11:55-1210 Initial Dept.]
1203:34	ID (B)	American eleven heavy turn right heading two two zero. [BOS 11:55-1210 Initial Dept.]
1203:37	AAL-11	two zero American eleven. [BOS 11:55-1210 Initial Dept.]
1204:27	ID (B)	American eleven heavy turn right heading two seven zero contact Boston approach one two seven point two good day. [BOS 11:55-1210 Initial Dept.]
1204:32	AAL-11	twenty seven two and two seventy American eleven so long. [BOS 11:55-1210 Initial Dept.]
1204:48	AAL-11	American eleven heavy with you passing through one zero thousand for one four thousand. [BOS 11:57-1210 Lincoln Dept.]
1204:52	SL	American eleven heavy Boston approach fly heading two seven zero. [BOS 11:57-1210 Lincoln Dept.]
1204:55	AAL-11	* seventy American eleven. [BOS 11:57-1210 L-incoln Dept.]
1205:14	SL	American eleven heavy contact Boston center one three three point four two. [BOS 11:57-1210 Lincoln Dept.]
1205:19	AAL-11	thirty three forty two so long American eleven. [BOS 11:57-1210 Lincoln Dept.]
1205:32	AAL-11	Boston center good morning American eleven with you passing through one one thousand for one four thousand. [BOS 1207-1214 Sector 47R]
1205:36	47R	American eleven Boston center good morning climb maintain flight level two three zero proceed direct CHESTER. [BOS 1207-1214 Sector 47R]

Flight 11

1205:41	AAL-11	two three zero direct CHESTER American eleven. [BOS 1207-1214 Sector 47R]
1208:47	47R	American eleven contact Boston center one two seven point eight two. [BOS 1207-1214 Sector 47R]
1208:50	AAL-11	twenty seven eighty two so long American eleven. [BOS 1207-1214 Sector 47R]
1209:17	AAL-11	Boston center good morning American eleven with you passing through one niner zero for two three zero. [BOS 1204-1233 Sector 46R]
1209:22	46R	American eleven Boston uh center roger climb and maintain level two eight zero. [BOS 1204-1233 Sector 46R]
1209:25	AAL-11	two eight zero American eleven. [BOS 1204-1233 Sector 46R]
1210:13	46R	American eleven climb maintain flight level two niner zero. [BOS 1204-1233 Sector 46R]
1210:15	AAL-11	niner zero American eleven. [BOS 1204-1233 Sector 46R]
1211:58	46R	American eleven your traffic is at uh two o'clock two zero miles southwest bound MD-80 three one oh. [BOS 1204-1233 Sector 46R]
121204	AAL-11	American eleven roger. [BOS 1204-1233 Sector 46R]
1213:29	46R	American eleven turn twenty degrees right. [BOS 1204-1233 Sector 46R]
1213:31	AAL-11	twenty right American eleven. [BOS 1204-1233 Sector 46R]
1213:47	46R	American eleven climb maintain flight level three five zero. [BOS 1204-1233 Sector 46R]
1213:57	46R	American eleven climb maintain flight level three five zero. [BOS 1204-1233 Sector 46R]
1214:08	46R	American eleven Boston. [BOS 1204-1233 Sector 46R]
1214:23	46R	American eleven Boston. [BOS 1204-1233 Sector 46R]
1214:33	46R	American one one uh the American on the frequency how do you hear me? [BOS 1204-1233 Sector 46R]
1215:15	46R	American eleven Boston. [BOS 1204-1233 Sector 46R]
1215:22	46R	American eleven if you hear Boston center ident. [BOS 1204-1233 Sector 46R]
1215:49	46R	American eleven if you hear Boston center ident please or acknowledge. [BOS 1204-1233 Sector 46R]
1216:32	46R	American eleven if you hear Boston center ah re-contact Boston Center on one two seven point eight two, that's American eleven one two seven eight two. [BOS 1204-1233 Sector 46R]
1217:05	46R	American eleven, American one one Boston. [BOS 1204-1233 Sector 46R]
1217:56	46R	American eleven if you hear Boston center ident please. [BOS 1204-1233 Sector 46R]
1218:56	46R	American eleven Boston. [BOS 1204-1233 Sector 46R]
1220:08	46R	American eleven American one one how do you hear the center? [BOS 1204-1233 Sector 46R]
1222:27	46R	American eleven Boston. [BOS 1204-1233 Sector 46R]
1224:33	46R	is that American eleven trying to call? [BOS 1204-1233 Sector 46R]
1224:36	AAL-11	**. [BOS 1204-1233 Sector 46R]
1224:38	AAL-11	we have some planes. just stay quiet and you'll be okay we are returning to the airport. [BOS 1204-1233 Sector 46R]
1224:46	46R	and uh who's trying to call me here? [BOS 1204-1233 Sector 46R]
1224:53	46R	American eleven are you trying to call? [BOS 1204-1233 Sector 46R]
1224:56	AAL-11	nobody move. everything will be okay. if you try to make any moves, you'll endanger yourself and the airplane. just stay quiet. [BOS 1204-1233 Sector 46R]

Flight 77

National Transportation Safety Board
Washington, DC 20594

Printed on : 11/23/2014 06:04:32 PM

Brief of Accident

Adopted 03/07/2006

DCA01MA064
File No. 19612

09/11/2001   Arlington, VA   Aircraft Reg No. N644AA   Time (Local):

	Fatal	Serious	Minor/None
Crew	6	0	0
Pass	58	0	0

Make/Model: Boeing/757-200
Engine Make/Model: Destroyed
Aircraft Damage: Destroyed
Number of Engines: Unk/Nr
Operating Certificate(s): Flag Carrier/Domestic
Name of Carrier: American Airlines
Type of Flight Operation: Scheduled; Domestic; Passenger Only
Reg. Flight Conducted Under: Part 121: Air Carrier

Last Depart. Point: WASHINGTON, DC
Destination: LOS ANGELES, CA
Airport Proximity:
Airport Name:
Runway Identification: Unk/Nr
Runway Length/Width (Ft): Unk/Nr
Runway Surface: Unk/Nr
Runway Surface Condition:

Condition of Light:
Weather Info Src:
Basic Weather:
Lowest Ceiling:
Visibility:
Wind Dir/Speed:
Temperature (°C): Unk/Nr
Precip/Obscuration:

Pilot-in-Command   Age:

Certificate(s)/Rating(s)
Airline Transport: Commercial; Multi-engine Land

Instrument Ratings

Flight Time (Hours)

Total All Aircraft: Unk/Nr
Last 90 Days: Unk/Nr
Total Make/Model: Unk/Nr
Total Instrument Time: Unk/Nr

*** Note: NTSB investigators traveled in support of this investigation and used data obtained from various sources to prepare this aircraft accident report. ***

The terrorist attacks of September 11, 2001 are under the jurisdiction of the Federal Bureau of Investigation. The Safety Board provided requested technical assistance to the FBI, and any material generated by the NTSB is under the control of the FBI. The Safety Board does not plan to issue a report or open a public docket.

NTSB: Brief

Flight 77

NATIONAL TRANSPORTATION SAFETY BOARD
Vehicle Recorders Division
Washington, D.C. 20594

December 21, 2001

Air Traffic Control Recording

Specialist's Report
by Joseph A. Gregor

A. ACCIDENT

Location:	The Pentagon, Arlington, VA
Date:	September 11, 2001
Time:[1]	
Aircraft:	Boeing 757-200
NTSB Number:	DCA01SA064

B. GROUP

N/A

C. SUMMARY

On September 11, 2001 American Airlines Flight 77, a Boeing 757 crashed into the Pentagon in Arlington, VA. A certified analog copy of air traffic control (ATC) transmissions recorded on September 11, 2001 at various tower, departure, and Air Route Traffic Control Center (ARTCC) positions along the route of flight was sent to the audio laboratory of the National Transportation Safety Board. These recordings were used to create an audio track and text transcript of the aircraft-ground communications from takeoff to accident time.

Flight 77

- ii -

D. DETAILS OF INVESTIGATION

Transmissions between the accident aircraft and ATC were recorded and an analog copy was sent to the Safety Board's audio laboratory. The tapes cover the following ATC positions and time periods:

Facility	Time Period[1] (UTC)	Position
IAD	1211 - 1226	LCW
	1215 – 1230	ND
	1218 – 1231	NH
ZDC	1220 – 1236	Sector 05R
ZDC	1226 – 1246	Sector 03R
ZID	1234 - 1309	HNN-R
	1249 - 1313	DAC-RA
	1249 - 1313	DAC-R

Sections of the tape recordings containing air-ground transmissions to and from the incident aircraft were digitized at a 22,050 Samples/second data rate and saved as standard Microsoft .wav files. Individual .wav files were combined into a single 43 minute 59 second long .wav file containing all transmissions to and from the incident aircraft from 1219:20 UTC (aircraft cleared for takeoff) to 1303:19 UTC. A transcript was obtained from the final composite recording. Times are approximate due to limitations inherent in the data obtained from the FAA.

Joseph A. Gregor
Electrical Engineer

Flight 77

Transcript of ATC communications with a Boeing B-757-200 (American Airlines flight 77) which crashed into the Pentagon in Arlington, VA on September 11, 2001.

LEGEND

AAL-77	Radio transmission from American B-767-200, flight 77
LCW	Radio transmission from Local Control West
ND	Radio transmission from North Departure
NH	Radio transmission from North High
05R	Radio transmission from Sector 05 Radar position
03R	Radio transmission from Sector 03 Radar position
HNN-R	Radio transmission from Henderson Radar position
DAC-RA	Radio transmission from DAC Radar Associate position
DAC-R	Radio transmission from DAC Radar position
*	Unintelligible word
#	Expletive
( )	Questionable insertion
[ ]	Editorial insertion
...	Pause
—	Interruption

Note 1: Times are expressed in universal coordinated time (UTC).

Note 2: Only radio transmissions to and from the accident aircraft were transcribed.

Note 3: Words shown with excess vowels, letters, or drawn out syllables are a phonetic representation of the words as spoken.

Flight 77

1219:20	LCW	American seventy seven your departure frequency will be one two five point zero five runway three zero cleared for take off. [IAD 1211-1226 LCW]
1219:27	AAL-77	twenty five point five cleared for take off runway ah three zero American seventy seven. [IAD 1211-1226 LCW]
1220:26	LCW	American seventy seven turn left heading two seven zero contact departure. [IAD 1211-1226 LCW]
1220:31	AAL-77	two seventy heading departure American seventy seven thanks sir good day. [IAD 1211-1226 LCW]
1220:43	ND	American seventy seven Dulles departure radar contact climb and maintain five thousand. [IAD 1215-1230 ND]
1220:47	AAL-77	five thousand American seventy seven. [IAD 1215-1230 ND]
1222:05	ND	American seventy seven climb and maintain one one thousand eleven thousand. [IAD 1215-1230 ND]
1222:08	AAL-77	up to one one thousand American seventy seven. [IAD 1215-1230 ND]
1223:23	ND	American seventy seven cleared direct LINDEN contact Dulles one one eight point six seven. [IAD 1215-1230 ND]
1223:28	AAL-77	direct LINDEN eighteen sixty seven American ah seventy seven **. [IAD 1215-1230 ND]
1223:43	AAL-77	* American ah seventy seven with you passing nine decimal one for eleven one one thousand. [IAD 1215-1230 NH]
1223:47	NH	American seven seven Dulles approach climb maintain one seven thousand. [IAD 1215-1230 NH]
1223:50	AAL-77	one seven thousand American seventy seven. [IAD 1215-1230 NH]
1225:33	NH	American seventy seven contact Washington center one two zero point six five good flight. [IAD 1215-1230 NH]
1225:37	AAL-77	twenty six five American seventy seven thank you maam good day. [IAD 1215-1230 NH]
1225:49	AAL-77	ah center American seventy seven with you passing one three decimal zero for one seven thousand. [ZDC 1220-1236 05R]
1225:57	05R	American seventy seven Washington center roger climb and maintain flight level two seven zero. [ZDC 1220-1236 05R]
1226:02	AAL-77	two seven zero American seventy seven. [ZDC 1220-1236 05R]
1230:38	05R	American seventy seven contact Washington center one three three point two seven. [ZDC 1220-1236 05R]
1230:42	AAL-77	ah thirty three twenty seven American seventy seven thanks sir good day. [ZDC 1220-1236 05R]
1231:05	AAL-77	* American seventy seven passing two five decimal one for two seven oh. [ZDC 1223-1246 03R]
1231:21	03R	American seventy seven ah climb, climb maintain flight level two niner zero sir. [ZDC 1226-1246 03R]
1231:27	AAL-77	two nine zero American seventy seven. [ZDC 1226-1246 03R]
1234:14	03R	American seventy seven turn twenty degrees right vector for your climb. [ZDC 1226-1246 03R]
1234:17	AAL-77	turn twenty right American seventy seven. [ZDC 1226-1246 03R]
1237:31	03R	American seventy seven recleared direct Charleston climb maintain cor -- correction recleared direct Henderson sir climb maintain.flight level three niner zero. [ZDC 1226-1246 03R]
1237:39	AAL-77	direct HENDERSON out of two nine for three nine oh requesting three five zero for a final American seventy seven. [ZDC 1226-1246 03R]
1237:55	AAL-77	center American ah seventy seven you copy request for three five zero as a final? [ZDC 1226-1246 03R]
1237:59	03R	American seventy seven ah roger maintain flight level three five zero I'll show that as your flinal. [ZDC 1226-1246 03R]

Flight 77

1238:03	AAL-77	ah three five zero for a final American seventy seven thank you sir. [ZDC 1226-1246 03R]
1239:30	03R	American seventy seven amend your altitude maintain flight level three three zero for traffic. [ZDC 1226-1246 03R]
1239:36	AAL-77	American seven seven stop at three three zero. [ZDC 1226-1246 03R]
1240:03	03R	American seventy seven contact Indy center one two zero point two seven. [ZDC 1226-1246 03R]
1240:06	AAL-77	twenty twenty seven American seventy seven thanks sir good day. [ZDC 1226-1246 03R]
1240:13	AAL-77	center American seventy seven with you level three three zero. [ZDC 1234-1409 HNN-R]
1240:15	HNN-R	American seventy seven Indy center roger squawk, three seven four three. [ZDC 1234-1409 HNN-R]
1240:19	AAL-77	three seven four three American seventy seven. [ZDC 1234-1409 HNN-R]
1243:51	HNN-R	American seventy seven climb and maintain flight level three five zero. [ZDC 1234-1409 HNN-R]
1243:55	AAL-77	thirty three, three five oh American seventy seven. [ZDC 1234-1409 HNN-R]
1247:16	HNN-R	American seventy seven turn ten degrees to the right vectors for traffic. [ZDC 1234-1409 HNN-R]
1247:20	AAL-77	ten right American seven seven. [ZDC 1234-1409 HNN-R]
1250:47	HNN-R	American seventy seven cleared direct ah FALMOUTH. [ZDC 1234-1409 HNN-R]
1250:51	AAL-77	ah direct FALMOUTH American seventy seven thanks. [ZDC 1234-1409 HNN-R]
1256:32	HNN-R	American seventy seven Indy. [ZDC 1234-1409 HNN-R]
1256:46	HNN-R	American seventy seven Indy. [ZDC 1234-1409 HNN-R]
1256:53	HNN-R	American seventy seven American Indy. [ZDC 1234-1409 HNN-R]
1257:12	HNN-R	American ah seventy seven American Indy radio check how do you read? [ZDC 1234-1409 HNN-R]
1257:27	HNN-R	American ah seventy seven American radio check how do you read? [ZDC 1234-1409 HNN-R]
1258:16	HNN-R	American seventy seven Indy radio check how do you read? [ZDC 1234-1409 HNN-R]
1258:20	DAC-RA	American seventy seven center. [ZDC 1249-1317 DAC-RA]
1258:41	HNN-R	American ah seventy seven ah Indy center how do you read? [ZDC 1234-1409 HNN-R]
1258:51	HNN-R	American seventy seven Indy radio check how do you read? [ZDC 1234-1409 HNN-R]
1259:32	DAC-RA	American seventy seven center. [ZDC 1249-1317 DAC-RA]
1300:25	HNN-R	American seventy seven Indy. [ZDC 1234-1409 HNN-R]
1300:56	DAC-RA	Indy center calling American seventy seven American seventy seven. [ZDC 1249-1317 DAC-RA]
1300:56	DAC-R	Indy center calling American seventy seven American seventy seven. [ZDC 1249-1317 DAC-R]
1303:06	HNN-R	American seventy seven Indy. [ZDC 1234-1409 HNN-R]
~1315:15	AAL-683	[called AAL-77 on guard at center request]. [ZDC 1249-1317 DAC-RA]

American Airlines Flight 587

Belle Harbor, New York

November 12, 2001

I N EARLY NOVEMBER 2001 THE International Airline Transport Association (IATA) Emergency Response Planners Working Group (ERPWG) was holding a conference in Rome, Italy. With the events of 9/11 still fresh in our minds, I had been asked to give a presentation on how American Airlines responded to this tragedy. I had never been to Rome, so I decided to take a few days of vacation time with my spouse after the conference to tour the city and relax before heading home. On November 12, 2001, we stopped at the front desk of our hotel to pick up the room key and the clerk said I had two messages. The first one said, "I am so sorry this has happened to you again." and the second said, "Please call your office immediately." We quickly walked to our room and I asked my spouse to turn on CNN while I called my office. At almost the same time someone answered the phone, the television news was reporting the crash of American Airlines Flight 587 from John F. Kennedy International Airport (JFK) to Santo Domingo (SDQ) in the Dominican Republic. The aircraft was an Airbus A300 -600 with 260 passengers and crewmembers. The plane crashed shortly after takeoff in a nearby neighborhood. All 260 on board the aircraft died as well as five people on the ground.

American Airlines was laying-off employees and the entire airline industry was struggling to stay alive since the 9/11 tragedy and now we had to respond to another accident. My boss, who was the Chief Accident Investigator for the airline, was flying over the Pacific Ocean on Qantas Airlines on his way to Sydney, Australia. American was able to reach the Qantas flight via Selective Calling (SELCAL) which provides the capability for ground to air communication. I had a Senior Analyst within our department who was away facilitating a class at Chicago O'Hare airport and only a Senior Analyst and support staff for our department at headquarters. Upon hearing of the accident, I dialed into our conference bridge line to stay on top of the activation process. My Senior Analyst at Headquarters and my Senior Analyst in Chicago were also on the call. We discussed our activation and deployment strategy and who would be stationed at the necessary locations for the response. I would fly from Rome to London's Heathrow airport and take a connecting flight to JFK. My spouse would travel with me to JFK and then fly home. My Senior Analyst at Headquarters would coordinate the activation and deployment process and then fly on the Go Team flight to JFK. My Senior Analyst who was in Chicago would head up the CARE HDQ response.

I contacted a colleague of mine with British Airways who was kind enough to meet us the next morning upon our arrival at Heathrow and walk us through Customs and Immigration. We had several hours before our flight to JFK and used the time to call our 24-hour bridge line to hear the latest update on the response. There were a number of international CARE Team members on our flight to JFK. Normally for a domestic accident we would utilize domestic team members. However, because there had been so many layoffs we had to utilize all locations from team members to ensure necessary manpower for the family assistance response.

Our Family Assistance Center (FAC) was going to be set up in the Ramada Inn Hotel JFK Airport. This hotel had been the host hotel for previous accidents such as Swissair 111, EGYPTAIR 990 and TWA 800. It made sense to utilize the same hotel. Unfortunately the city of New York did not agree with us. When I left Rome for JFK, we were scheduled to use the Ramada Inn. When I landed at JFK, our Family Assistance Center had moved to the Javits Convention Center in New York City. American Airlines had reserved hundreds of rooms at the Ramada at JFK and a few other hotels close by. Because we had reserved such a large number of rooms, which had been removed from the hotel inventory, the hotels would not release us from the contracts. Every day we coordinated bus transportation to and from the JFK airport hotels to the Javits Convention Center for over 450 CARE Team members. Flexibility was key to the response of Flight 587, especially after our FAC was changed. It is imperative emergency response plans be flexible to withstand outside influences you may encounter. The priority was the Family Assistance Center; the procedure was changed to meet the priority of the families and of the City. In addition to the NYC Family Assistance Center, CARE Command Centers were established in Santo Domingo the destination point of the flight, Miami, Florida because it was a connecting city to Santo Domingo, DFW Airport, and London, England.

Eight weeks had passed since the tragic events of 9/11. Most of us were still physically and emotionally exhausted from the response. I am not sure where the responders found their energy, but they did. Adrenaline is very powerful. There were many challenges with the response to this accident. One of which was issuing an advance payment check for $25,000 to the legal next of kin for those killed on the aircraft and on the ground. The checks were actually flown on the Go Team flight but were not issued quickly enough according to the families. After several days waiting for the advance payment, local newspapers were quoting family members and others as saying American Airlines were racists because in previous accidents checks were issued faster. Because a large majority of passengers were Dominican, the thought was, American held back on the payments. Nothing could have been farther from the truth. CARE Team members were tasked with working with their families to determine the legal next of kin so a check could be issued. However, complicated family dynamics contributed to the inability of many families to determine and advise who was the legal next of kin. This significantly contributed to the delay in checks being issued. It had nothing to do with the nationality of passengers or crew.

The Family Assistance Center was large enough to hold over 1,000 family members, all the CARE Team members, American Red Cross representatives, State Police Officers, New York City representatives and countless others. In hindsight it was a good decision to move the FAC, however it still would have been nice to be included in the decision so we did not have to bus hundreds of employees each day.

Family assistance briefings were conducted daily. Initially there were challenges with the translation services provided for those who did not speak English. An American Airlines representative would translate and family members would share with us afterwards if the translation was not accurate. After several complaints, we had a family member representative translate the briefings and the American Airlines employees who spoke Spanish said the translation was inaccurate. Eventually we found a translator from the United Nations to translate all content provided during the family assistance briefings. Remember, I discussed translation services in Chapter 4, Flight 965.

Flight 587 Images

COURTESY OF THE: NTSB

While we had made gains with our Spanish-speaking volunteers, it was still not enough. Do not make the same mistake. Research potential translation service providers now. Trust me, it will be needed.

The Medical Examiner's office for New York City was overwhelmed. They were processing remains from the two World Trade Center towers and the planes which had been flown into them. Now they had another mass casualty situation to process. During a family assistance briefing the Medical Examiner advised how long it would take to positively identify all on board the aircraft and those who died on the ground. He said it would take approximately 10 days. The problem with giving such a distinct timeline is people expect you to deliver on your promise. You can imagine how angry families were when the due date arrived and no one had been positively identified. The aircraft crashed on November 12 and the last remains would be released for burial just days before Christmas, much longer than the 10 days originally promised.

At one point during the response I flew to Santo Domingo to see how the team was doing. During my visit I received a call from the Medical Examiner's Office in NYC informing me a body had wrongfully been sent to a family in Santo Domingo. I was asked to share this with the family, apologize on the Medical Examiner's behalf and advise the correct remains would be quickly transported. To make matters worse, the family had just buried their presumed loved one the day I received the information from the NYC Medical Examiner's Office. I was not particularly comfortable talking with the family because this was not an airline mistake. I offered to fly a representative of the Medical Examiner's office to Santo Domingo and have them meet with the family in person to explain what occurred and that is what we did. I understand mistakes happen, even one as horrible as this.

The FAC in New York City was open far longer than needed. The first family assistance briefing held on November 12 had over 1,000 family members in attendance. By the time the FAC closed in early December, we had less than 20 family members a day in attendance. At this point the NTSB briefings had stopped and the Medical Examiner was releasing remains on a regular basis. CARE Team Members were working with their family members in person at the family's home or on the telephone. However, New York City management would not allow the center to close. As a matter of fact, the City mandated a temporary center be opened in the Washington Heights area where a large number of the families were from. The American Red Cross (ARC), working with American Airlines searched for a location convenient for family members. Once the location was determined, the structure was cleaned, phone lines and computer lines were run and furniture brought in. We complied with the request of the City and only one person, who was not even a family member, came to the center. The person was a passenger for a future flight wanting to change their seat assignment. I appreciate what the City was trying to accomplish, however it simply was not necessary given the support the families already had received from the CARE Team Members assigned to them.

When the topic of the site visit was being discussed, the National Transportation Safety Board requested the site visit take place first followed by a memorial service. This was an established practice from previous accidents and made the most sense. Family members may become emotional during the site visit and having the memorial service afterwards helps to calm some of the emotion. The City of New York did not follow the recommended practice. CARE Team Members worked with their families to determine the number of family members desiring to attend the site visit. Remember 260 passengers and crew were on board the plane and five killed on the ground.

Over 3,750 people attended the site visit. American Airlines working with the city of New York coordinated the movement of approximately 100 buses to facilitate the transportation of all the family members. The memorial service was during the afternoon and was followed by the site visit. As anticipated, individual family members became very emotional, many cried and several even fainted. The American Red Cross was on hand, along with paramedics, to provide emotional support and medical assistance if needed. Wanting to help those grieving, neighbors within the area of the crash site brought cookies, hot chocolate and other refreshments for those attending the site visit. Buses would arrive on adjacent streets, the passengers would

Flight 587

COURTESY OF THE: NTSB

get off the bus, view the site, return to the bus and go home. The next buses would pull forward and the process would start again. It took almost four hours to complete the site visit. It was dark and cold when the last family members boarded the bus for home.

A challenge we had not encountered before was the transportation of so many remains to a single destination. Many of the passengers were from Santo Domingo. There were times when multiple remains were released for burial by the Medical Examiner. American Airlines largest aircraft, the Boeing 777 (B-777), could only accommodate so many at one time. In addition, the B-777 was not the aircraft used on all flights from JFK to SDQ. We coordinated with our SOC for additional wide-body aircraft and extra flights in order to transport all of the remains. The passengers and crew were transported with respect, dignity and sensitivity.

It is always a cultural challenge during a mass casualty event to understand the nuance of varied burial customs. When the first passengers were released for burial, several of the bodies were sent to Santo Domingo for interment. Team members came back to the command center in horror of what they experienced. While a family was gracious to allow the CARE team members to attend the funeral service, the team members were shocked at what happened. Apparently the custom in parts of the Dominican Republic was for family members to desecrate the casket before being lowered into the ground. The purpose for this is to lessen the likelihood of grave robbers digging up the casket, removing the body and stealing the casket for resell. From the team members experience we were able to brief all of our team on what they may experience when attending a funeral service and validate for them this was the normal practice and not to be alarmed. With the number of countries airlines fly to these days, it is very difficult for an airline to navigate all of the worlds various burial practices. Even those in the field of mortuary services cannot possibly be familiar with all customs.

One day in the Joint Family Support Operation Center (JFSOC) a Commissioner from the Mayor's office was yelling at me because he believed there were family members who did not have CARE Team members assigned. I asked him multiple times who the family members were not receiving assistance and he was not able to respond. I advised him we had over 450 team members on the ground to support our response to the crash of Flight 587 and our records indicated all family members had at least two team members assigned to them. He never mentioned it again.

However, there were many Commissioners from the Mayor's office, there were Assistant Commissioners and other representatives and many wanted to dictate how the operation should be run. I had a conversation with one of the Commissioners about the site visit and he told me how it was going to run. I told him, with all due respect, I did not report to him and my obligation was to the National Transportation Safety Board and the families of those impacted by the accident. When it was time to close the Family Assistance Center, a City representative approached me with an invoice for the cost of operating the center while we were there. It was not an itemized invoice and I would not sign it. I advised him there were things acquired during the response the airline had no say about and we would not consider paying an invoice unless it was itemized and reviewed by our risk management department. Procedurally, all of our responders from the airline and even outside organizations in most cases maintained a log of expenses for insurance purposes. Our team members kept a log, I kept a log, and I certainly expected the City of New York to keep a log. He was not happy with my decision but it was the right thing to do.

Flight 587 Images

COURTESY OF THE: NTSB

AP Images

Overall, the response to Flight 587 was relatively smooth and well staffed. There were challenges along the way; however, most of these challenges were not seen by the families and were handled professionally between all the stakeholders. Whatever the challenges the airline had with the City of New York, the response would never have been as smooth or as successful without the support of the many departments within the Mayor's office. Not everyone is going to agree in a disaster response but everyone does agree on trying to do the right thing for those impacted by the disaster.

Just before Easter 2002 the Medical Examiner's Office contacted American Airlines to advise they had newly identified remains for over 170 bodies from Flight 587. While all the passengers and crew had already been positively identified and interred, these were additional remains for the families to consider for internment. We asked for the names of the passengers and crew for these remains and the city would not provide them until all the families had been notified. We maintained once the families were notified, the airline would receive calls for assistance with transportation of the additional remains. We needed the names so we could properly assist those who called. Without the names, we could not verify if the individual calling had actually received additional remains of their loved one.

American set up a small command center in New York City and Santa Domingo and assisted family members with transportation of the remains and transportation for them as well to inter the remains. We worked very closely with the necessary departments to take care of the families, answer their questions and provide the necessary assistance.

Lessons Learned

1 **Flexibility.** I know I have said this over and over again but it is so true. In short, focus on Priorities not Procedures™.

2 **Vendor management.** Are the vendors you have in place able to carry out their work in each of the locations where you may need their service?

3 **Translation services.** Translation services were needed for the Family Assistance Center briefings. It is critical you have a neutral third party to translate the briefings. Having a neutral party will help lesson the opportunity of translation bias.

4 **Document your work.** Keep good records of questions you answer, actions you take and any equipment procured. This documentation will be vital when the response is over and the insurance group needs to review costs for reimbursement.

5 **Repatriation of remains.** How will you transport remains for repatriation? Even if you have a third party vendor to assist you with this task, they may not have the means to transport numerous remains if you are responding to a mass casualty event. Understand now what your organization's capabilities are with regards to transport of the remains.

6 **Communication devices.** How will you provide communication devices such as mobile phones or pagers to your team members? Establish a relationship with mobile phone providers now and create a minimum equipment list of what your needs are for initial deployment.

7 **Prepaid phone cards.** Procure prepaid phone cards for family members to use so they do not have to use their mobile minutes or incur long distance phone charges using their landline.

8 **Location based knowledge.** It is critical for an organization to understand, especially at their largest cities of operation, any nuances with regards to how the airport and/or city may respond to an aviation accident or other mass casualty event. Where are the overlaps in the response? Are there any conflicts? Resolve these now.

Flight 587

Executive Summary

On November 12, 2001, about 0916:15 eastern standard time, American Airlines flight 587, an Airbus Industrie A300-605R, N14053, crashed into a residential area of Belle Harbor, New York, shortly after takeoff from John F. Kennedy International Airport, Jamaica, New York. Flight 587 was a regularly scheduled passenger flight to Las Americas International Airport, Santo Domingo, Dominican Republic, with 2 flight crewmembers, 7 flight attendants, and 251 passengers aboard the airplane. The airplane's vertical stabilizer and rudder separated in flight and were found in Jamaica Bay, about 1 mile north of the main wreckage site. The airplane's engines subsequently separated in flight and were found several blocks north and east of the main wreckage site. All 260 people aboard the airplane and 5 people on the ground were killed, and the airplane was destroyed by impact forces and a postcrash fire. Flight 587 was operating under the provisions of 14 *Code of Federal Regulations* Part 121 on an instrument flight rules flight plan. Visual meteorological conditions prevailed at the time of the accident.

The National Transportation Safety Board determines that the probable cause of this accident was the in-flight separation of the vertical stabilizer as a result of the loads beyond ultimate design that were created by the first officer's unnecessary and excessive rudder pedal inputs. Contributing to these rudder pedal inputs were characteristics of the Airbus A300-600 rudder system design and elements of the American Airlines Advanced Aircraft Maneuvering Program.

The safety issues discussed in this report focus on characteristics of the A300-600 rudder control system design, A300-600 rudder pedal inputs at high airspeeds, aircraft-pilot coupling, flight operations at or below an airplane's design maneuvering speed, and upset recovery training programs. Safety recommendations concerning these issues are addressed to the Federal Aviation Administration and the Direction Général de l'Aviation Civile.

Flight 587

National Transportation Safety Board
Washington, DC 20594

Brief of Accident

Adopted 04/14/2005

Printed on : 11/23/2014 05:58:32 PM

DCA02MA001
File No. 17648

11/12/2001   Belle Harbor ,NY   Aircraft Reg No. N14053   Time (Local) 09:16 EST

	Make/Model:	Airbus Industrie/A300B4-605R
	Engine Make/Model:	General Electric / CF6
	Aircraft Damage:	Destroyed
	Number of Engines:	2
	Operating Certificate(s):	Flag Carrier/Domestic
	Name of Carrier	AMERICAN AIRLINES INC
	Type of Flight Operation:	Scheduled; International; Passenger Only
	Reg. Flight Conducted Under:	Part 121: Air Carrier

	Fatal	Serious	Minor/None
Crew	9	0	0
Pass	251	0	0
Other	5	0	0

Last Depart. Point:	New York City, NY
Destination:	Santo Domingo
Airport Proximity:	Off Airport/Airstrip

Condition of Light: Day
Weather Info Src: Weather Observation Facility
Basic Weather: Visual Conditions
Lowest Ceiling: None
Visibility: 10.00 SM
Wind Dir/Speed: 270 / 008 kts
Temperature (°C): 6
Precip/Obscuration:

Pilot-in-Command   Age: 42

Certificate(s)/Rating(s)
Airline Transport: Multi-engine Land

Instrument Ratings
Airplane

Flight Time (Hours)

Total All Aircraft: 8050
Last 90 Days: 146
Total Make/Model: Unk/Nr
Total Instrument Time: Unk/Nr

*** Note: NTSB investigators traveled in support of this investigation and used data obtained from various sources to prepare this aircraft accident report. ***

The Board's full report is available at http://www.ntsb.gov/publictn/publictn.htm.

On November 12, 2001, about 0916:15 eastern standard time, American Airlines flight 587, an Airbus Industrie A300-605R, N14053, crashed into a residential area of Belle Harbor, New York, shortly after takeoff from John F. Kennedy International Airport, Jamaica, New York. Flight 587 was a regularly scheduled passenger flight to Las Americas International Airport, Santo Domingo, Dominican Republic, with 2 flight crewmembers, 7 flight attendants, and 251 passengers aboard the airplane. The airplane's vertical stabilizer and rudder separated in flight and were found in Jamaica Bay, about 1 mile north of the main wreckage site. The airplane's engines subsequently separated in flight and were found several blocks north and east of the main wreckage site. All 260 people aboard the airplane and 5 people on the ground were killed, and the airplane was destroyed by impact forces and a postcrash fire. Flight 587 was operating under the provisions of 14 Code of Federal Regulations Part 121 on an instrument flight rules flight plan. Visual meteorological conditions prevailed at the time of the accident.

Corporate Airlines Flight 5966 D.B.A. American Connection

October 19, 2004
Kirksville, Missouri

OCTOBER 19, 2004, AMERICAN CONNECTION Flight 5966 flying from Lambert St. Louis International Airport to Kirksville, Missouri crashed short of the runway killing 11 passengers and two pilots. There were two survivors with serious injuries. The aircraft and the crew were part of Corporate Airlines. They were one of three airlines flying as American Connection airlines, a feeder carrier for American Airlines.

The American Airlines Emergency Response and CARE Department worked very closely with the emergency response representatives of the three carriers, which comprised American Connection, as to how an emergency would be handled. American Airlines would provide station emergency response guidance, telephone enquiry centre assistance, as well as CARE Team Members to assist the survivors and the families of those who died.

Within the airline industry there are various Alliances, Codeshare partnerships and other arrangements air carriers make with each other with regards to marketing and other aspects of the partnership. It would be better to establish the parameters of what each partner will provide in terms of emergency response and family assistance support before an accident occurs. Then you must educate all the key stakeholders within your organization about exactly what your response to a partner's emergency will be. Nothing fails faster than a plan no one knew anything about. There must be corporate buy-in with regards to mutual aid. I have experienced situations where some departments within an airline said they would only respond to an event within their organization not a partner's. However, if your company, airline or otherwise, is establishing joint ventures with other organizations or, if your airline is part of an Alliance or Codeshare arrangement it is imperative all stakeholders know what is expected when an emergency occurs. Corporate buy-in is a must!

Corporate Airlines Dispatch notified American of the accident and AA notified key department stakeholders including CARE. Because this accident occurred after normal business hours, we first met via conference call. We determined the level of the event and agreed to set up the command center at SOC. On my way to the command center I notified the National Transportation Safety Board Transportation Disaster Assistance Division of the accident and our pending deployment. I also advised I would send the flight manifest once I arrived at SOC. Because we had shared with them in advance what we were prepared to do for a partner, The NTSB understood AA would respond to one of our partner carriers in an emergency. The last thing we needed was any surprises at the accident city as to why we were there. In short, communicate your plans with internal and external stakeholders.

My team assembled in the CARE command center, which was located next to SOC. We began the notification of local DFW CARE

Team volunteers, updated the CARE hotline with the accident information and began to work through our deployment procedures. In addition, we would work with the local Kirksville station employees to assist them as they worked through their emergency procedure checklists.

There were a number of people on the conference bridge line asking other stakeholders for pieces of information. At the same time station personnel were asking questions, someone unaffiliated with the emergency response department was answering the station questions incorrectly. I interrupted the person who was providing the incorrect information and introduced myself as the Manager of the Emergency Response department. I then provided the station with the accurate information they needed which was provided in their Station Emergency Procedures Manual (SEPM). Later I would find out the person responding was an Officer with American Airlines and he was none too pleased I interrupted him. I have a respect for someone's position but in an emergency response, providing incorrect information, especially when you do not even represent the safety organization, is ill advised. At the very least, there should be a side conversation, offline from the bridge call to clarify or confirm the procedure. I still believe today, as I did in 2004, individuals who are not trained, educated, or work in the emergency response field, should convey their advice to the leader of the response before simply announcing it on an open bridge line.

The Kirksville airport would close due to the accident and would remain closed for several days while the investigation into what happened took place. This complicated the deployment of the AA Go Team while we searched for the nearest airport to Kirksville. The closest airport was approximately three hours away by car. In addition, the airport could not handle an American Airlines jet but could

Flight 5966 Images

AP Images

accommodate an American Eagle regional jet. The airline's Go Kits had each been weighed to determine the weight and balance calculations for departure. The kits contained needed material to establish a local command center and Family Assistance Center. Items such as printers, phones, shredders, office supplies and other equipment. The kits were too large for the regional jet and had to be broken down into smaller containers to accommodate the aircraft. Once we arrived at our destination, airport buses would transport the Go Team members and CARE Team Members to the accident city.

Corporate Airlines was the certificate holder for the operation of this flight. Because American Airlines and American Eagle Airlines were not the airline certificate holders for this accident, services provided to the Corporate Airlines investigative team would be guidance only. American Airlines and American Eagle investigators would not be allowed on scene as they were not party to the investigation. In addition, AA Corporate Communications representatives were on scene in Kirksville to assist Corporate Airlines with press releases and media coverage. Station emergency response and family assistance services are permitted by anyone the air carrier designates. According to the Emergency Response Agreement, American Airlines would provide station response guidance and family assistance as well as, open their TEC. Because there were only 15 people on board the aircraft and, partly because the airport was closed, the manpower needed to respond to survivors and the families was not as high as it had been in previous accidents.

Kirksville, Missouri is a small town with limited hotels and conference room space. In addition, it was homecoming weekend for the local university and many of the hotel accommodations were already taken. Normally we would try to have one team member per room so the team member could relax and rest before they continued their work with the family. With this particular response we would need to have two team members to a guest room due to the fact accommodations were taken. The only hotel with guestrooms and conference space was the Days Inn Hotel. After that, the closest hotel was miles away. The staff of the hotel was excellent. The manager, front desk clerks, restaurant team and housekeeping went out of their way to help the families who traveled to Kirksville and assist the CARE Team Members staying at the hotel.

The NTSB did their best to maximize the use of the facilities provided. Unfortunately, the hotel did not have the technology available to always accommodate their needs. For example, the NTSB would have a conference bridge line available for family members who could not or chose not to come to Kirksville. The bridge line provided a means by which family members could call in and hear the information being provided during the family assistance briefing. The hotel did not have the necessary equipment to do this. Instead, the Polycom unit was duct taped to a podium and the built-in speaker left on so the callers on the other end of the line could hear what was being said. Primitive, yes! But it worked.

The wooded area where the plane crashed was very muddy and, initially, was considered unsafe for there to be a site visit by the families. As the days went on, the ground began to dry and it was determined safe to have the site visit. The family members and their CARE Team Members would be bussed to the site where each could pay their respects. Any work being performed at the site was discontinued out of respect for the families. Bales of hay formed a makeshift barrier between the accident location and where the families stood. Many people choose to lay flowers, leave pictures, or place a card on the haystacks to honor their loved one.

During the response the President and the Director of Safety for Corporate Airlines were always available to answer any questions.

If anyone from the leadership team had a question about what was appropriate in terms of actions taken on behalf of the family being served we would consult with Corporate Airlines and with their insurer, who was on site, to determine the best response.

The crash of American Connection flight 5966 was one of the first accidents since the passage of the Aviation Disaster Family Assistance Act of 1996 where the partner of the operating carrier performed family assistance. Thankfully, American and Corporate Airlines had built a strong relationship and had decided on a response plan before anything ever happened.

During our response to this event, an NTSB Board meeting as to the findings of the crash of AA Flight 587 was on the calendar to take place in late October in Washington, D.C. We had to coordinate our manpower to accommodate a new provision that had been legislated in 2003. Vision 100-Century of Aviation Reauthorization Act Sec. 809 mandated the following:

> (18) An assurance that, in the case of an accident in which the National Transportation Safety Board conducts a public hearing or comparable proceeding at a location greater than 80 miles from the accident site, the air carrier will ensure that the proceeding is made available simultaneously by electronic means at a location open to the public at both the origin city and destination city of the air carrier's flight if that city is located in the United States.

Flight 587 originated in the United States and was destined for the Dominican Republic. American Airlines was responsible for obtaining a venue where the families and the public could gather to watch the Board proceedings taking place in Washington, D.C. Thankfully, we had already taken care of the logistics for this before the Kirksville accident occurred. However, it still meant a loss of manpower from my staff as someone from my department needed to be in New York to ensure everything at the venue where the NTSB Board proceedings were being shown took place as scheduled.

The response to Flight 5966 was not like any of the other accidents I had responded to in the past with regards to the number of families involved. Not many family members traveled to the accident location as in accidents past as many chose to talk with the Telephone Enquiry Centre CARE Team Member instead. We did not deploy a large number of CARE Team Members because the shear number of passengers and crew was small. Additionally, there was very little space to house everyone.

In this response, the overall activation time for Family Assistance was relatively short, due in part, to the size of the aircraft involved being smaller than a full size passenger jet. However, regardless of the size of the aircraft or the number of souls on board, the feelings, activities, grief, anger and everything else associated with the response were virtually the same.

Lessons Learned

1   **Partnership.** Coordinate with your transportation partners or organizational partners in advance of an accident. Within the airline industry there are so many Alliances and Codeshare agreements established it might become very confusing as to who is responsible for the response. Establish the parameters of what each partner will provide in terms of support. Then educate all the necessary stakeholders of the plan. Nothing fails faster than a plan people do not know anything about.

2   **Corporate buy-in.** Obtain corporate buy-in to the agreed upon mutual aid. All stakeholders need to be on board when you are responding on behalf of a partner company/organization.

3   **Government agencies.** If your organization is prepared to respond on behalf of a partner, contact the necessary government agencies to advise them of your response agreement so they understand ahead of time to expect you on scene until the accident organization team arrives.

4   **Go-Kits.** If you maintain Go-Kits, be careful that your kits are not too big. They need to be small enough to fit the cargo hold of the smallest aircraft you may utilize. In addition, each kit should be weighed and the weight posted on it. This step will help the ground crew determine a more accurate weight and balance for the GO Team flight.

Flight 5966

Executive Summary

On October 19, 2004, about 1937 central daylight time, Corporate Airlines (doing business as American Connection) flight 5966, a BAE Systems BAE-J3201, N875JX, struck trees on final approach and crashed short of runway 36 at the Kirksville Regional Airport (IRK), Kirksville, Missouri. The flight was operating under the provisions of 14 *Code of Federal Regulations* Part 121 as a scheduled passenger flight from Lambert-St. Louis International Airport, in St. Louis, Missouri, to IRK. The captain, first officer, and 11 of the 13 passengers were fatally injured, and 2 passengers received serious injuries. The airplane was destroyed by impact and a postimpact fire. Night instrument meteorological conditions (IMC) prevailed at the time of the accident, and the flight operated on an instrument flight rules flight plan.

The National Transportation Safety Board determines that the probable cause of the accident was the pilots' failure to follow established procedures and properly conduct a nonprecision instrument approach at night in IMC, including their descent below the minimum descent altitude (MDA) before required visual cues were available (which continued unmoderated until the airplane struck the trees) and their failure to adhere to the established division of duties between the flying and nonflying (monitoring) pilot.

Contributing to the accident was the pilots' failure to make standard callouts and the current Federal Aviation Regulations that allow pilots to descend below the MDA into a region in which safe obstacle clearance is not assured based upon seeing only the airport approach lights. The pilots' unprofessional behavior during the flight and their fatigue likely contributed to their degraded performance.

The safety issues in this report focus on operational and human factors issues, including the pilots' professionalism and sterile cockpit procedures, nonprecision instrument approach procedures, flight and duty time regulations, fatigue, and flight data/image recorder requirements.

Flight 5966

National Transportation Safety Board
Washington, DC 20594

Brief of Accident

Adopted 01/24/2006

Printed on : 11/23/2014 06:07:28 PM

DCA05MA004
File No. 19619

10/19/2004	Kirksville ,MO	Aircraft Reg No. N875JX	Time (Local): 19:37 CDT

Make/Model: British Aerospace/Jetstream 32
Engine Make/Model: Garrett-Airesearch / TPE331
Aircraft Damage: Destroyed
Number of Engines: 2
Operating Certificate(s): Flag Carrier/Domestic
Name of Carrier: CORPORATE AIRLINES
Type of Flight Operation: Scheduled; Domestic; Passenger Only
Reg. Flight Conducted Under: Part 121: Air Carrier

	Fatal	Serious	Minor/None
Crew	2	0	0
Pass	11	2	0

Last Depart. Point: St. Louis, MO
Destination: Same as Accident/Incident Location
Airport Proximity: Off Airport/Airstrip

Condition of Light: Night/Dark
Weather Info Src: Weather Observation Facility
Basic Weather: Instrument Conditions
Lowest Ceiling: 300 Ft. AGL, Overcast
Visibility: 3.00 SM
Wind Dir/Speed: 020 / 006 kts
Temperature (°C): 9
Precip/Obscuration: No Precipitation; Unknown Obscuration

Pilot-in-Command   Age: 48

Certificate(s)/Rating(s)
Airline Transport: Commercial: Multi-engine Land: Single-engine Land

Instrument Ratings
Airplane

Flight Time (Hours)

Total All Aircraft: 4234
Last 90 Days: 191
Total Make/Model: 2510
Total Instrument Time: Unk/Nr

*** Note: NTSB investigators traveled in support of this investigation and used data obtained from various sources to prepare this aircraft accident report. ***

The Board's full report is available at http://www.ntsb.gov/publictn/publictn.htm. The Aircraft Accident Report number is NTSB/AAR-06/01.

On October 19, 2004, about 1937 central daylight time, Corporate Airlines (doing business as American Connection) flight 5966, a BAE Systems BAE-J3201 N875JX, struck trees on final approach and crashed short of runway 36 at Kirksville Regional Airport (IRK), Kirksville, Missouri. The flight was operating under the provisions of 14 Code of Federal Regulations Part 121 as a scheduled passenger flight from Lambert-St. Louis International Airport, in St. Louis, Missouri, to IRK. The captain, first officer, and 11 of the 13 passengers were fatally injured, and 2 passengers received serious injuries. The airplane was destroyed by impact and a postimpact fire. Night instrument meteorological conditions (IMC) prevailed at the time of the accident, and the flight operated on an instrument flight rules flight plan.
Updated at Jul 24 2009 1:17PM

Conclusion

When responding to an aviation disaster, family assistance is a delicate process. It is an intuitive balance between sometimes-insensitive procedures and regulations and the dramatic variables of emotions and obstacles. Through my experiences I have found people can handle the truth regardless of how difficult the truth is to hear. Oftentimes it is our own fear that prohibits us from sharing difficult news because we do not want to bring additional pain to the survivor or the family. However, when we are not transparent and do not share information the family so desperately wants, it is exactly what we do, add more pain.

As human beings responding to people who have experienced an aviation accident or lost a family member because of one, the most compassionate act we can do is be empathetic and most of all honest.

As a CARE Team Member and Leader, I have seen the best of humanity. Hundreds of team members willing to put their fear aside to help people they have never met during one of the most difficult times in their lives. I have witnessed people who have lost a loved one or survived a horrific plane crash open their hearts for help.

Over the years I have learned many aspects of emergency response, from developing checklists, creating exercises and drills to organizing an efficient team structure. The one aspect of responding to mass casualty events I did not learn from a book or a class is how resilient and courageous human beings are in the time of crisis. People can handle the truth, they will survive and so will we.

Acronyms for Resilience

Acronym	Definition
AA	American Airlines
ADFAA	Aviation Disaster Family Assistance Act of 1996
AMR	NYSE Stock Trading Symbol for American Airlines
ARC	American Red Cross
ASAP	Aviation Safety Action Program
CARE	Customer Assistance Relief Effort
CISD	Critical Incident Stress Debrief
CLO	Alfonso Bonilla Aragón Airport
CTM	CARE Team member
CVR	Cockpit Voice Recorder
d.b.a.	Doing Business As
DCA	Ronald Reagan Washington National Airport
DFW	Dallas Fort Worth International Airport
DMORT	Disaster Mortuary Operational Response Team
DMS	Docket Management System
DNA	Deoxyribonucleic Acid
DoD	Department of Defense
DOS	Department of State
DOT	Department of Transportation
EAP	Employee Assistance Program
ERP	Emergency Response Planning
ERPWG	Emergency Response Planners Working Group
EST	Eastern Standard Time
FAA	Federal Aviation Administration
FAC	Family Assistance Center
FBI	Federal Bureau of Investigation
FDR	Flight Deck Recorder
FMS	Flight Management System
FOQA	Flight Operations Quality Assurance
HDQ	Headquarters building for American Airlines
HIPPA	Health Insurance Portability and Accountability Act
HNL	Honolulu Airport
IAD	Washington Dulles International Airport
IATA	International Air Transport Association
ICAO	International Civil Aviation Organization
ICS	Incident Command System
IN	Indiana
IND	Indianapolis Airport
IRS	Internal Revenue Service
JFK	John F. Kennedy International Airport
JFSOC	Joint Family Support Operations Center

Acronyms for Resilience

LGA	LaGuardia Airport, New York City, New York
LIT	Bill and Hillary Clinton National Airport/Adams Field
M.E.	Medical Examinar
MAS	Master of Aeronautical Science
MIA	Miami International Airport
NC	North Carolina
NTSB	National Transportation Safety Board
OPED	Organization Performance and Employee Development
ORD	Chicago O'Hare Airport
PACC	Passenger Assistance Command Center
RDU	Raleigh Durham International Airport
SDQ	Santo Domingo
SELCAL	Selective Calling
SEPM	Station Emergency Procedures Manual
SMS	Safety Management System
SOC	System Operations Control
SRO	Southern Reservations Office for American Airlines
TEC	Telephone Enquiry Centre
The Act	The Aviation Disaster Family Assistance Act of 1996
TX	Texas
UA	United Airlines
VST	Victim Support Task
WARN	Worker Adjustment and Retraining Notification Act

Appendix:

A Brief History of Aviation Disaster Response

Jennifer Stansberry Miller, a clinical social worker and family member, continues to advance and support the subject matter of family assistance through a nonprofit organization, *Connections, A Disaster Resource Consortium*. With permission, I have provided several pages from the *Connections* website explaining why The Aviation Disaster Family Assistance Act of 1996 (The Act) was needed:

The Aviation Disaster Family Assistance Act of 1996 was born after areas of critical importance were poorly coordinated or mismanaged following several commercial aviation disasters that occurred between the late 1980's and the mid 1990's. Air carriers, local authorities and federal agencies lacked a comprehensive and compassionate response, leaving family members of those who were killed in accidents with nowhere to turn. Communication from the airlines lacked vital information loved ones were seeking. The victim identification process fell short. Families received human remains that had been misidentified. Burials of unidentified human remains were conducted in several disasters without the families' knowledge. Families learned that identifiable personal effects of their loved ones were intentionally destroyed after the accident rather than being returned. Following one accident, families discovered personal effects and human remains in a dumpster. In other accidents, families and friends who visited some sites months after the mitigation was completed discovered human remains, personal effects, and plane parts.

In 1994, victims' family members and survivors from several aviation disasters came together to advocate for a coordinated and humanitarian approach by the aviation industry and government in working with individuals impacted by a commercial aviation disaster. Families and survivors took their stories to Washington, D.C. seeking change.

On June 20, 1995, family members and survivors from American Eagle flight 4184, US Air flight 427, US Air flight 405, and US Air flight 5050, brought those concerns to a meeting hosted by the National Transportation Safety Board (NTSB) and the Department of Transportation (DOT). The meeting allowed the NTSB and DOT to understand the common issues and develop a plan to improve assistance to family members and survivors. The meeting attendees created an outline of 14 points of concern experienced by victims' families and aviation disaster survivors. Families and survivors continued their push by participating in congressional meetings and testifying before the United States Congress.

In 1996, two all-fatal commercial aviation disasters, ValuJet flight 592 and TWA flight 800, again highlighted the overwhelming need for a coordinated crisis response plan within the aviation industry. On July 31, 1996, the Aviation Disaster Family Act (HR3923, 104th Congress) was introduced in the United States Congress by then Congressman Bud Shuster (R-PA) and 42 cosponsors.

On September 6, 1996, President Clinton signed an executive memorandum to seven federal agencies that tasked the NTSB to be the lead agency in coordinating the federal response to major aviation and transportation accidents. The order cited the importance of improving the capacity within the federal government in addressing the needs of families of victims of transportation accidents.

The Aviation Disaster Family Assistance Act was passed in the House of Representatives on September 18, 1996 by a vote of 401 to 4. Prior to the bill's passage Rep. Shuster stated, "So it is my hope . . . our colleagues on the other side of the Capitol will indeed move these very, very important pieces of aviation legislation, not the least of which is this very important family bill that is before us today."

Surrounded by victims' family members and survivors, President Clinton signed the Federal Aviation Administration (FAA) Reauthorization Act of 1996 into law on October 9, 1996. Included in this, under Title VII was Family Assistance — Aviation Disaster Family Assistance Act of 1996. President Clinton remarked: "And I thank all the family members who are here for your efforts to go beyond your own personal suffering to make something positive happen for our country in the future."

The legislation required the creation of a Task Force comprised of aviation disaster survivors and victims' family members, federal agencies, congressional leaders, attorneys, and the aviation industry. They were charged with addressing the concerns that led to the legislation and offer recommendations on how to mitigate such actions in the future. At the conclusion of their eight months of work, they issued 61 recommendations on how to best meet the needs of aviation disaster victims' families. The recommendations addressed a variety of family member concerns, from enlisting the

American Red Cross to provide disaster mental health support, to a 45-day moratorium baring attorney's from soliciting victims' families, to guiding the NTSB to brief families prior to the media about their progress of the investigation and early response efforts, to the consultation of common burials prior to completion. Over the next few months, those recommendations evolved into a systematic model that guided the industry and resulted in the development of the Federal Family Assistance Plan for Aviation Disasters.

Additionally, the Act forged a new responsibility for the NTSB to create the Transportation Disaster Assistance (TDA) Division within the agency. The TDA was charged with coordinating the resources of federal, state, and local agencies, transportation carriers, and the American Red Cross, to meet the needs of family members and survivors following a transportation accident. TDA also serves as the primary resource for investigative information for family members and survivors.

Over the years, the Act has influenced creation of the Foreign Air Carrier Support Act of 1997 and the Rail Passenger Disaster Family Assistance Act of 2008. In 2013, the footprint of the Act appeared once again when the International Civil Aviation Organization (ICAO) created the "ICAO Policy on Assistance to Aircraft Victims and Their Families," which guides their 191 member states on effectively addressing the needs of family members for information and access to services.

The history of aviation accident family assistance reflects the capacity of the human spirit rising from tragedy and underscores the power in building relationships between individuals, industry and government. In the words of Joe Lychner, a TWA flight 800 family member who served on the Task Force, "Working together, we can make things better."

About the Author

Ken Jenkins is a highly experienced transportation disaster response consultant, responding to emergencies ranging from the 9/11 terrorist attacks, to the crash of Asiana Flight 214 in San Francisco. Ken directed over five hundred CARE Team Members deployed following the 9/11 attacks and the Crash of American Airlines Flight 587 crash later that year. All told, Ken has responded to 12 major accidents and numerous lesser emergencies. Ken has a Master's Degree (With Distinction) in Aeronautical Science from Embry-Riddle Aeronautical University and currently resides in Dallas, TX.

For more information, visit Ken at:
www.kenjenkinsllc.com
email: kjenkins@kenjenkinsllc.com
twitter: @kenjenkinsllc

CPSIA information can be obtained
at www.ICGtesting.com
Printed in the USA
FSOW03n1905180515
7111FS